STAR QUEST I

SPACEJACK!

STAR QUEST I

SPACEJACK!

TERRANCE DICKS

A Target Book
published by
the Paperback Division of
W. H. ALLEN & CO. LTD

A Target Book
Published in 1979
by the Paperback Division of W. H. Allen & Co. Ltd
A Howard & Wyndham Company
44 Hill Street, London W1X 8LB
Second Impression 1979

First published in Great Britain by
W. H. Allen & Co. Ltd, 1978

Printed in Great Britain by
Richard Clay (The Chaucer Press) Ltd
Bungay, Suffolk
ISBN 0 426 20050 0

Contents

I

Fire in the Sky

They were talking about life on other planets the night it happened. The night that was to be their last on Earth . . .

There were three of them, Jan, Kevin and Anna, and they were camping out on a deserted bit of Salisbury Plain, close to Stonehenge. Despite different looks, and different nationalities, all three were cousins.

Anna was Swedish, dark-haired, thin and wiry.

Jan was American, tall, broad-shouldered, with bright blue eyes and hair so fair it looked almost white. He never tired of teasing Anna about the fact that he looked far more Swedish than she did. (Since Anna, like many Swedes, spoke perfect English, most people assumed at first that Jan was the Swedish one.)

Kevin, their English host, was medium-sized, brown-haired, and as he cheerfully admitted, 'just sort of average-looking'.

They weren't sure exactly how they were related to each other. 'Kind of fourth cousins once or twice removed,' was how Jan put it. All three were descended from three Swedish brothers. Two of the brothers had left Sweden for America in the eighteen-fifties. They'd stopped off in England on the way and the younger had promptly fallen in love, married, and settled down.

The second brother had travelled on to America, eventually reaching Minnesota, where he too married.

The third had stayed in Sweden on the family farm.

All three brothers had lots of children, all *their* children had lots more. By now, the Petersons were a huge three-country family. The different branches of the family kept in touch, and the younger relatives in particular visited each other frequently.

This year Kevin's parents had invited Jan and Anna to spend the summer with them, and Kevin, an only child, had suddenly found himself overwhelmed with company. Luckily he found he liked both his cousins, though Jan's cheery self-confidence could be a bit overpowering.

The idea was that Kevin should show his foreign cousins the usual tourist sights. But for once England had produced a real heat-wave, and it wasn't long before trailing round the Tower and Westminster Abbey with a mob of roasting tourists got pretty unbearable.

So Kevin suggested a cycle-camping holiday. He hadn't really expected Jan to agree. 'Everyone knows you Yanks spend all your time riding around in Cadillacs.'

Jan was indignant. Cycling was very big in America just now, and he had a perfectly good bike at home. As for riding everywhere in cars . . . 'Have you ever been back-packing along the Appalachian Trail? Or white-water canoeing in Oregon? Or pony-trekking in New Mexico?' Jan had, and a cycling holiday was fine by him. 'That is if you can do much cycling in a country this size. Couple of days and you'd probably ride off the edge!'

They'd hired bikes for Jan and Anna and set off, and

now they were sprawling around a little campfire on a hot summer night, looking up at the stars and arguing about UFOs—Unidentified Flying Objects.

As usually happened, Jan and Kevin were on opposite sides, Jan openly scornful, Kevin a firm believer. Anna was neutral. She lay looking up at the stars, dropping in the occasional remark just to keep things going.

So far Jan was getting the best of it. He'd rushed into the argument with his usual cheerful confidence. 'It's all a lot of crazy nonsense. People see weather balloons, observation satellites, sun flashing on the wings of a plane . . . Most of those UFO nuts are pretty freaked out to start with—they just let their imaginations run away with them.'

'Oh yes?' said Kevin quietly. 'Like those US Airforce pilots in nineteen forty-eight? Three Mustang fighters spotted a UFO and chased after it—the lead plane blew up when it got too close.' Kevin paused for breath. 'There was a whole spate of UFO sightings round about that time, most of them by pilots in your own Air Force. Not particularly nervous types, I should have thought. Then there was that BOAC pilot who spotted a space ship and six smaller ones when he was flying over Canada. And *four* American policemen spotted a UFO over Ohio and chased it in their police cars!'

Kevin went on to give a string of other UFO sightings over the years, all with sane, sensible-sounding witnesses, all difficult to explain away. Jan shook his head, baffled but still not convinced. Anna couldn't help feeling rather sorry for him. He'd obviously made the mistake of tangling with an expert.

'So why don't these aliens make contact?' asked Jan belligerently. 'Why not just land on the White House lawn and say, "Take me to your leader?" '

'Perhaps they don't want to—perhaps they're just observing us.'

'Perhaps, perhaps, Kev. I still say there's no proof...' The argument raged on.

Anna stared sleepily up at the blaze of stars. She'd heard enough by now, and she was just about to suggest they all shut up and went to bed when she saw something that put the whole question of UFOs on a very different level. 'Hey, you two, stop jabbering and look!' She pointed upwards. An arrow of light was flashing across the sky.

Silently they studied the moving streak. It was surrounded by a hazy glow and it seemed jagged, somehow dart-like. The object streaked down through the sky and disappeared below the horizon, in the direction of Stonehenge.

Suddenly Jan shouted, 'Look—there's another one!'

A second object was hurtling down through the night sky as if in pursuit of the first. This second space ship was larger, round rather than rocket-like, very much the shape of the conventional 'flying saucer'. It was surrounded by the same hazy glow as the first, but they could make out a row of windows around the side, and a raised central dome on the upper surface. They stared in utter astonishment as it sped silently across the sky and vanished below the horizon.

Kevin shook his head in amazement. It was all very well defending UFOs in theory, but seeing one . . . 'It's a UFO,' he whispered. 'A genuine UFO!'

'*Two* UFOs' corrected Jan. 'Looks as if one was chasing the other.' He grinned at Kevin and slapped him on the back. 'Cheer up cousin, you are about to get famous!'

'Am I,' said Kevin cynically.

Jan stared at him. 'Well of course you are. We saw them, didn't we? We all did.'

'We saw them all right! Do you think anyone will believe us?'

'Of course,' said Anna impatiently. 'There are three of us, and we will all say the same thing.'

'What about those pilots, and those policemen, all the other people who saw UFOs? Did anyone believe them? Three kids camping alone at night? They'll say we were seeing things. They'll say it was a weather balloon, or a satellite or the planet Venus . . .'

Anna tried to imagine telling her mother and father she'd seen flying saucers on her English camping holiday. 'Yes, dear, how nice,' they'd say. She could just hear them telling their friends about her wonderful imagination. 'Perhaps Kevin is right. We'd better just forget the whole thing.'

Jan started stamping out the fire. 'Those UFOs weren't just flitting through the sky. They were *landing*. I'm going to find out where—and why! Who's coming with me?'

2

The Aliens

Jan swung one leg over his bike-saddle. 'Come on you two—what are you waiting for?'

'We can't just go rushing off in the dark,' protested Anna. 'We'll all get lost.'

'Still, Jan's right,' said Kevin suddenly. 'We've *got* to follow this up.' He went to his saddle-bag, fished out a compass and an ordnance survey map, and aligned map and compass. 'Now they disappeared just to the left of that clump of trees . . . .' He looked up. 'I reckon they'll come down somewhere here, close to Stonehenge!' Kevin folded the map and reached for his bike. 'Coming, Anna? Or are you going to stay behind and mind the camp?'

The suggestion that she ought to take a safe back seat was too much for Anna. 'Of course I'm coming.' She ran to her bike. 'Though what good is it going to do? I mean even if we do get a closer look, people still won't believe us.'

'Good thinking,' said Jan. He reached down into his saddle-bag, pulled out his camera-case and slung it round his neck. 'This'll do it. Clear, unfaked, close-up pictures. Let them explain that away. Now then, are we going to stand here telling each other how clever we are, or are we going to get the show on the road?'

'Okay, okay,' said Kevin cheerfully. 'No harm in a

little advance planning. Right—follow me!' Compass cupped in one hand, Kevin wobbled off, Jan and Anna close behind him.

It was like a kind of mad cross-country cycle race, thought Anna, as she followed the two red rear-lights bobbing ahead of her. Kevin kept their route ruthlessly on his compass-bearing and they were soon forced to leave the path for the open plain. They jolted over tussocky grass, dismounting to drag the bikes through hedges, across ditches and over fences.

The journey seemed to go on for ages, though in their slow cross-country progress they couldn't have covered more than a few miles. Kevin came to a halt. 'Look!' The ground rose steadily in front of them—and from the other side of the hill there came a glow. They had reached their target.

Jan laid his bike carefully on the ground. 'Come on,' he whispered, and set off up the hill on foot. Kevin and Anna followed him. Moving as quietly as they could, they made their way up the rise. The glow grew steadily brighter as they neared the top. They came over the crest of the rise, and before them lay Stonehenge. It was bathed in the eerie glow from the space ship that had landed close beside it. Silvery figures moved about under the great stones.

Kevin studied the scene below him, determined to memorise every detail. First the space ship. It was long and black, triangular in its overall shape, standing upright on its tail like a conventional rocket. Short stubby wings flared out from the side—it occurred to Kevin that they might be retractable, designed only for use in a planetary atmosphere.

Beside him Jan raised his camera and began taking shot after shot of the alien space ship.

Kevin turned his attention to the figures moving among the stones. They were man-shaped, not particularly large, and they wore one-piece space-suits in some silvery material. Their boots and gauntlets were black. Wide black belts around their waists held a variety of pouches and containers. Strangely they were helmetless. They all seemed to have thin, pale faces with close-cropped yellow hair.

It occurred to Kevin that the space ship might not be from some other planet at all. The astronauts looked human enough. Could this be an experimental model on a secret test flight? Somehow he doubted it. The ship seemed more advanced than anything yet developed on Earth. And if the Americans or the Russians had come up with a revolutionary space ship, why use it to go poking round Stonehenge in the middle of the night?

Kevin turned his attention back to the silver figures. There were three of them, and they were examining the stone pillars one by one. One would sweep the surface of the pillar with what looked like a giant metal torch, moving a reddish light-beam over the entire surface. The second stood watching a smaller, box-like apparatus in his hands. The third figure held a rifle-shaped device with bulbous stock and a short, thick barrel. He swung the weapon warily to and fro as if keeping watch. Hidden in the darkness, the watchers studied the mysterious scene. 'What are they looking for?' whispered Anna.

'Only one way to find out,' said Jan softly. 'We'll have

to get closer.' Crouching low, he began running towards the space ship.

'Come back you idiot!' hissed Kevin, but Jan was already on his way. Kevin turned to Anna. 'Stay here —I'll get him.' He ran after Jan.

Anna wanted to follow, but common sense told her the more of them rushing about near the space ship, the greater the chances of being seen. Suppose these mysterious aliens didn't like being spied on?

Kevin found his cousin just beyond the edge of the circle of light cast by the space ship. Jan had wriggled as close to Stonehenge as he dared. Now he lay propped up on his elbows, taking shot after shot of the aliens and their mysterious activities.

Kevin dropped down beside him. 'What do you think you're doing?'

Jan grinned. 'Just getting a few close-ups. I wonder what those guys are up to? They've covered pretty well all the major stones by now.'

Forgetting he was there to bring Jan back, Kevin joined him in watching the aliens. They were gathered round one of the smaller megaliths, following the same unvarying routine. One swept the red light-beam over the surface, the second stood watching, the third kept guard.

Jan gave Kevin a nudge. 'I think they've hit the jackpot!'

The alien astronauts were crowding round the stone. As the light-beam swept across the surface something was happening!

Tiny points of light were appearing on the stone, dozens of them, connected by thin glowing lines. It looked oddly familiar and all at once Kevin realised what it reminded him of—one of those diagrams in astronomy books, showing you the constellations. 'It's a map,' he whispered. 'Some kind of star chart!'

Jan was already on his feet again, moving closer to the stone, using the last of his film to get a close-up of the glowing map.

Anna meanwhile was getting really worried. Jan and Kevin were very close to the aliens by now. If one of them turned . . .

Anna felt the ground beneath shake. Something was moving towards her from the other side of the slope. Judging by the thud of its footsteps, it was something very large indeed.

She felt trapped like a rabbit in a cornfield. If she moved forward she'd run straight into the aliens from the space ship. Move back and she'd be going towards those approaching footsteps. Glancing fearfully over her shoulder, she crouched down, not daring to move.

An astonishing figure had appeared on the skyline behind her. It was enormous, at least three metres high, and it wore a space-suit made from some brown, leather-like material. The head was bare, and the sight of the creature's face made Anna gasp with horror. It was a hideous, almost misshapen face like that of a Neanderthal cave man. The underhung jaw was huge and brutal, and dark eyes glared from beneath a low bony forehead. One massive paw clutched a strange-looking pistol.

For a moment the creature paused, swinging the savage head to and fro, sniffing the air through its broad, flat nostrils. It made a beckoning gesture, and a second figure moved up to stand beside it. This one was much smaller, below human height, but immensely broad and powerful. It was similarly dressed and armed, and had a broad, flat, troll-like face.

Anna was frozen with terror. 'A giant and a dwarf,' she thought dazedly. 'What next?'

Her question was answered all too soon. A third creature appeared—and this one was pure nightmare.

It was shaped rather like a giant octopus—an octopus adapted to living on land. Long tentacles supported a round bulbous body, and two enormous golden eyes reflected the light from the glowing space ship. A webbing harness was strapped about its body, and it was carrying a pistol-like weapon in one of its tentacles.

This third apparition was too much for Anna. She jumped to her feet yelling, 'Jan! Kev! Look out—look behind you!'

Several things happened more or less at once. Jan and Kevin turned—and so did the aliens examining the stone megalith. At the sight of the newcomers, the one with the rifle raised his weapon and opened fire. There was a fierce glow as enegy-bolts whizzed through the air.

Jan and Kevin threw themselves down—but Anna was still on her feet running towards them. Something crackled fiercely within inches of her head, and a massive electric shock slammed her unconscious to the ground. The giant alien was already running forward, and Anna collapsed at his feet.

'Anna's hurt,' yelled Jan. He jumped up and ran back to her. One of the silver-clad aliens raised his gun and fired, and Jan toppled to the ground.

Kevin flung himself down, and the battle raged over his head. The giant and the dwarf were returning fire now, and the air crackled with purple rays. He saw the octopus-creature touch a control on its belt-harness and immediately a shimmering veil of blue light encased the octopus-alien, his two companions and Anna as well—a barrier against which the energy-bolts of their attackers sizzled in vain.

Under cover of this protective shield the strange trio began making a retreat. Kevin saw the giant pick up Anna's unconscious body, tossing it over his shoulder like an empty sack. 'Hey, come back!' he yelled. The three aliens vanished back into the night.

Kevin was about to follow when he saw two of the black-clad aliens dragging his cousin's unconcsious body towards the space ship.

Kevin was paralysed with indecision as his friends were carried off in opposite directions. His instinct was to go after Anna, but she had already disappeared and he could still see Jan. The black-and-silver aliens looked more or less human. Perhaps he could persuade them to let Jan go. Better still they might even help him to rescue Anna . . . All this went through Kevin's mind in seconds. He jumped up and ran towards the space ship. A ramp was sliding out, and a door had opened. The two aliens were dragging Jan up the ramp, while the third stood guard. As he reached him Kevin yelled, 'Please, you've got to help me. They've taken my cousin.' The alien ignored him. Jan was almost inside the ship by now. Kevin forced his way up the ramp and tried to pull him back. The sentry clubbed him down from behind with the butt of his laser.

For a moment the aliens looked down at Kevin's body. The leader gave a brief command, and the sentry dragged him inside the ship. The hatch slid closed, the ramp retracted, and in an eerie silence the glowing ship hurtled up into the night sky. It flashed across the darkness, then suddenly winked into extinction.

3

Captives of the Kaldor

The dwarf-like alien called Tell watched the fiery spot until it disappeared. He knew that the Kaldor ship had left Earth space for the space/time continuum. It would flash back into normal space millions of light-years away. His stocky body slumped despairingly. 'They are already in hyper-drive, Osar. We have lost them.'

'I should have stayed on the ship,' said the octopus-like Osar agitatedly. 'I am a navigator, it is not my function to land on alien worlds. Our tracking beam was not locked on—without their jump co-ordinates we shall never find them again.'

Tell looked up at the great stones towering above him. 'We should scan these stones—they must have been searching for something . . .'

Osar was horrified, waving his tentacles in protest. 'Our presence here breaks the most solemn ruling of the League. Unless we go now there will be Contact—and that is utterly forbidden.'

'Contact has already taken place,' said Tell. 'Kidnapping too. The Kaldor took two young humans captive.'

Osar scuttled forward with the peculiar sideways gait of his people, and stared up at the great stone circle. 'Why?' he hissed angrily. 'Why take the humans captive? Why come here at all?'

Tell hunched his wide shoulders. 'They seek some fragment of the Old Wisdom—something that will serve their lust for power.' He returned to his argument. 'They were scanning these stones—stones left here by the Old Ones. We have equipment in the ship. If I go back and fetch it . . .'

Osar swayed his body from side to side in the gesture that meant refusal. 'Who knows what frequency they were using? You could seek for eternity without success. The invisibility-shield on the ship is draining our power reserves. If we stay longer there'll be too little power to make the Jump.'

The huge Neanderthal figure of Garm loomed up out of the darkness. 'The Earth girl is hurt. I cannot tell how badly. We must take her to the ship.'

Osar's tentacles moved in renewed agitation. 'Is it not bad enough that we are here? Must we now turn kidnapper like the Kaldor? If the Council hear of this . . . Leave her and come away.'

'We broke the Council's law by coming here,' said Garm calmly. 'If we leave the girl she may die. I shall take her to the ship.' He turned away, Osar scuttling after him.

Tell grinned wryly. Osar's race had a combination of mental brilliance and physical sensitivity that made them incomparable star navigators. Unfortunately it also made them excessively temperamental and highly nervous.

Tell turned for a last regretful look at the towering stones. They held some great secret, he was sure of that. If only they could stay and search . . . But Osar was right, it was time to go.

As he moved away, Tell's foot struck some small loose object. He picked it up and studied it, trying to work out its function. Controls, a lens . . . a primitive video-recording device by the looks of it. He slipped it inside his tunic and hurried after the others.

He found them waiting nearby, close to a saucer-shaped depression in the plain. It was a strange depression; one that had not been there a short time before. There was nothing to be seen in the hollow, yet on the shallow bowl of its floor, grasses and shrubs were flattened. Anyone trying to cross the hollow would have been thrown back by an invisible force.

Osar was dancing on his tentacle tips with impatience. 'Coming with us after all, are you?' He curled up one tentacle to adjust a control on his harness. Dazzling light filled the hollow as the invisibility shield was turned off and the ship shimmered slowly into view. It was saucer-shaped, with a raised round dome in the centre, the standard starship often seen from Earth. A hatch opened, a ramp slid out and all three entered the ship, Garm carrying the unconscious girl. The hatch closed and a moment later the ship rose silently into the air and vanished into the clouds.

Next day there were numerous reports of flying saucers, seen over Salisbury Plain. A farmer up all night with a calving cow, a married couple driving back after a party in London, a policeman cycling home after late duty, these and others reported seeing a saucer-shaped craft pursuing a dart-shaped one through the sky. Some people claimed to have seen them twice, as if both ships had actually landed and taken off.

One of the local papers featured the story, and there was a paragraph or two in the national press. The day after the whole thing was forgotten.

It wasn't until some time later that anyone realised that three young people were missing. Kevin and his cousins hadn't been following any special route, and they'd been keeping in touch with Kevin's family by the occasional phone call or postcard. Then someone found three bikes and an abandoned camp-site close to Stonehenge. Kevin's diary was in the tent and the police contacted his parents.

There was a full-scale search after that, police, army, civilian volunteers . . . They found nothing. A police spokesman said, 'It's as if they'd disappeared from the face of the Earth.' An enterprising local reporter pointed out that the young people had vanished on the night of the UFO sightings, and suggested there might be some connection. His editor told him to stick to the facts, and the story was quashed. Jan, Kevin and Anna had vanished.

Anna Peterson was having a nightmare. She dreamed she lay stretched out on a couch, with a giant hovering over her. The giant held a strangely-shaped instrument in his enormous hand, moving it slowly about her head. Anna struggled to wake up—and realised she was awake, and the nightmare was real. She tried to sit up, drawing breath for a scream, but an enormous hand pressed her back. She heard a deep reassuring voice, not with her ears, but somehow inside her head. 'Do not be afraid. No one will harm you.'

For a moment Anna was reassured, but then she

saw the second shape hovering close by. The bulbous body balanced on its sinuous tentacles, the great golden eyes . . . with a scream of horror she fainted dead away.

Garm looked down at the Earth girl for a moment, then headed for the control room. Osar had arrived ahead of him, twittering with indignation. Tell was doing his best to soothe him down. The cruiser was on automatic, speeding away from Earth in the general direction of Mars.

Tell looked up. 'How is our passenger?'

'Better than I had feared. She was caught by the fringe of a blaster ray—there is shock, but no real damage.' Garm smiled. 'I'm afraid that Osar frightened her!'

Osar waved a disdainful tentacle towards the controls. 'Let us reverse course immediately and carry her back to Earth. She is quite uncivilised.'

Garm shook his head. 'No, not yet. Place us in orbit around the fourth planet for a time. When she recovers I should like to talk to her. Perhaps she knows something that might help us.'

'A primitive girl from Old Earth?' Osar was incredulous. 'What can she possibly know?'

The acceleration couch creaked beneath Garm's enormous weight. He yawned. 'Perhaps she knows why the Kaldor kidnapped her friends . . .'

Jan and Kevin too had a nightmare awakening but their nightmare was harsher, and went on for much longer. They awoke to find themselves strapped to the walls of a metal cell. A man in a black-and-silver uniform shouted questions at them in a language they didn't understand.

The questioning went on and on. Their interrogator took some time to realise that they couldn't give the answers because they didn't understand the questions. He seemed to lose his temper and struck Jan savagely across the face, bringing blood to his lips. It was a serious mistake. The blow brought Jan back to full consciousness—and to a state of furious rage. With a yell of anger he snapped the bonds that held him to the wall and flung himself upon his tormentor. Grabbing the alien with his left hand, Jan delivered a thump with his right that sent him flying across the room.

Black-clad figures descended on Jan from all sides and he disappeared beneath a pile of attacking bodies. Somehow he managed to shake them off, rising to his feet and lashing about him with a series of blows that sent his attackers reeling. Despite his comparative youth Jan was exceptionally big and powerful, and in his berserk fury he didn't even seem to notice the blows of his opponents.

Still fastened to the metal wall, Kevin looked on helplessly as Jan flung his attackers about the room. For a moment it actually seemed as if Jan would succeed in disposing of all his attackers, but in the end there were too many for him. While four of the black-clad aliens held his arms, a fifth slipped behind him and clubbed him savagely across the head with the butt of a blaster. Half-dazed, Jan was dragged across the room and fastened back into place, this time with stronger bonds.

The aliens began restoring the interrogation-room to

order—Jan had almost wrecked it in his struggle. Smashed and overturned equipment was righted and replaced, bruised and semi-conscious crewmen carried out. When things were more or less straight, another alien entered.

He looked uncannily like the first one, with the same slight wiry build and cruel hawk-like face. He spoke briefly to the interrogator, who came forward with a metal helmet in his hands and fitted it over Jan's head, ignoring his struggles. A flex connected the helmet to a nearby control-panel. Once the helmet was in place, the interrogator crossed to the controls, made adjustments and threw a switch. To Kevin's horror, Jan arched his back, gave a choking scream and slumped unconscious in his bonds.

The alien at the console frowned, as though some minor experiment had gone irritatingly wrong. He lifted the helmet from Jan's head and carried it across to Kevin.

Kevin tossed his head wildly from side to side trying to avoid the helmet, but the alien jammed it brutally into place. Again the man crossed to the controls, made adjustments and pulled the switch. Kevin too screamed as a searing jolt hammered through his brain. It was as though his mind was a sheet of wax upon which someone had slammed down a giant metal stamp. He was sick and dizzy from the shock, but unlike Jan he managed to remain conscious, perhaps because his mind was more flexible. The helmet was lifted from his head and the questions began again. But now there was a difference. He could understand them.

Somehow that shattering mental jolt had blasted an

entire new language into his brain. His grasp was shaky at first and he could only get the general drift of questions. But as the interrogation went on, he could understand more and more.

'Who?' his interrogator was demanding. 'Who are you? Why do you watch us? Why do you help the League?'

Gradually Kevin began to work out what must have happened. His captors had got the idea that he and Jan were part of the second group of alien astronauts, the ones whose appearance had frightened Anna. Interrupted in their scanning of Stonehenge, they had registered Jan, Kevin, Anna and the three newcomers all more or less at once, and had assumed they were together—an idea which had been strengthened when Anna was carried off.

Kevin did his best to sort things out. 'We're nothing to do with those others,' he shouted. 'We were just observers, do you understand? Observers!'

'You lie,' shouted the interrogator. 'The League have summoned the help of Earth. We know that some of you still have the Old Wisdom. You will help them to destroy us!'

The questioning went on and on. The subordinate asked all the questions while the second alien, obviously the leader, listened impassively. A complicated combination of dials and electrodes was clipped to Kevin's forehead and wrists. He was asked the same questions all over again. Defiantly he shouted the same answers, while the leader studied the flickering needles on the dials. At last he nodded, satisfied, and the questioning stopped.

The two black-clad figures moved to one side, and Kevin slumped back as if barely conscious. The aliens began a low-voiced conference. Kevin strained to hear what they were talking about. He heard mention of 'the quest' and gathered that they were in search of some great secret. There was talk of the Old Wisdom, and of some mysterious group of humans who might, or might not, help them. Kevin's use of the word 'observer' seemed to cause them some concern—they seemed to be wondering if he could be more important than he appeared.

Finally the interrogator said something about 'useless—safer to eject.' Kevin shuddered, realising that the alien was casually suggesting they be ejected from the ship to die a hideous death. In the icy vacuum of space their bodies would simply explode. To his vast relief he saw the leader shake his head. Kevin caught only a few words of his low-voiced reply. There was something about the League. 'They saw us, they will tell the Council. Keep prisoner . . . bargain . . . hostage . . . 'And then 'Observers—observers from Earth—may have important knowledge.'

It seemed the second group of aliens, the League, knew they were on this space ship and might make trouble if they were killed . . . Moreover, the leader thought they might still be of some use to him. Kevin didn't fully understand, but he didn't need to. He was happy to be alive.

4

Empire in the Stars

Inside Anna's head a deep voice was saying, 'Open your mind. No one will harm you.'

She felt a kind of mental pressure, as though someone was trying to force a way into her brain. She sat up, gasping, but a giant hand forced her back. 'Try to open the channels of your mind.' Anna stopped resisting and immediately information poured into her mind in a swirling flood. Words, sounds, images, faster and faster, until at last the rushing stream of data overwhelmed her and she lost consciousness.

When she awoke for the second time the giant had gone, and the dwarf was sitting beside her. 'My name is Tell,' he said. 'And what is yours, my lady?'

'Anna.' She sat upright, staring at him. 'I understand you. I answered you!'

'That is so. You are now fluent in Basic Pan-galactic, the language spoken, or at least understood, by every intelligent life-form in the galaxy.'

'How? How did I learn so quickly?'

'By mind-link. Garm is a telepath. The information came straight from his brain to yours.'

'Who are you? Where am I—and what am I doing here? Who were those people at Stonehenge? What's happened to Jan and Kev?'

Tell held up his hand, his eyes sparkling with amusement. 'If you will stop the flow of questions long enough to hear my answers . . . My name is Tell. My large friend Garm you have already met. The third of us is called Osar. You hurt his feelings badly when you fainted—he has a very sensitive nature.'

'I'm sorry—it's just that he isn't . . .'

Tell's ugly face was curiously attractive when he smiled. 'Human? Nor am I, Princess, not fully human, and nor is Garm, though unlike Osar we are descended from human stock. The agents of the League come in many shapes.'

'The League? What League?'

'The League of Sentient Life Forms, of course—an alliance of all intelligent beings in this Galaxy.'

Anna was still thinking of something the little alien had said a moment ago. 'Did you just say two of you were descended from human beings?'

'Of course. We are the heirs of the First Galactic Empire of Man.'

'But humans have never had a galactic empire. We've only just reached our own moon!'

'Listen, Princess, and I will tell you the True History of Man.'

Anna forced herself to sit back and listen, as Tell unfolded an amazing story. According to him, Earth was now entering its second civilisation. Man had first evolved on Earth millions of years before present-day humans now believed. 'You were the most advanced species in the Galaxy in those days. In an amazingly short time you evolved a technological civilisation, discovered space flight, developed the hyper-drive, and spread out all over the Galaxy, colonising and conquering more than a million worlds.'

'You mean there are other worlds like Earth? Worlds where men can live and breathe the air?'

'Others?' Tell laughed. 'The Galaxy you call the Milky Way holds more than a hundred thousand *million* stars. Say one in a thousand is circled by an E-type planet . . .'

'A hundred million Earths,' said Anna softly.

Tell shrugged. 'In fact one in a thousand is too low an estimate. Much of the Galaxy is still unexplored. Even the First Empire took in only part of it.'

'What happened to this First Empire? Why don't we know about it now?'

'It grew and grew until it collapsed from within. There were over a million worlds in the Empire towards the end. Who can administer an Empire of such size? Who can even count the worlds that pay tribute?' Tell sighed. 'The Empire fell. Much of the Galaxy fell with it, reverting to barbarism.'

'Including Earth?'

'Earth was the first. Its decline was total and complete. Atomic wars, plagues, devastation. The shape of Earth was altered, whole continents rose and fell. Man went back to the caves, where he crouched gnawing a bone, worshipping the stars that once he ruled.' Tell paused, pleased with this poetic turn of phrase.

'Did this happen on all the other worlds?'

'Things varied greatly. Some planets destroyed themselves in interstellar wars, on others civilisation continued to flourish. My own was one such world,' Tell concluded proudly.

'Then why didn't you help us?' demanded Anna indignantly.

'Because you were lost!'

'Lost? How can the Earth have been lost?'

'A hundred million habitable worlds, remember? Some civilised, some barbaric, others somewhere in between. Some devastated by atomic wars, others still empty of intelligent life. Nearly all of them inhabited by humans or humanoids. Who could tell which was the true original Earth?'

'But you know now,' said Anna. 'Eventually you found us.'

'The discovery was made some thirty Earth-cycles ago. There was great excitement in the Galaxy when the home-world of man was rediscovered.'

'And that's when all the UFO business started,' said Anna excitedly. 'You found us, and you came to take a look at us!'

'Indeed we did! Starships were popping out of hyper-space all over your solar system. Every world with star flight came to take a look at Old Earth. There was chaos. Time and again our ships were seen by the Earth people. Your atmospheric flyers came too close and were exploded by protective force-fields. Your water-borne vessels disappeared. Unauthorised Contact was made. Extra-terrestrials landed and were seen by humans. Earth people were taken to other planets. It was a disaster!'

Anna nodded, remembering Kevin's stories of the great UFO boom of the 'fifties, a time when scarcely a day passed without some kind of sighting. 'And then it all tailed off. What happened?'

'That was the League,' said Tell proudly. 'There was a risk that great harm would be done to Earth, that its natural redevelopment would be interfered with. The League declared Earth a forbidden planet. Occasional overflights are permitted for observation purposes, but that is all.'

'So the visits stopped? No more UFOs—or hardly any. What about tonight?'

'Law-abiding planets obey the rule of the League—but there are others—like the Kaldor.'

'The ones we saw examining Stonehenge? What did they want?'

Tell paused, as if gathering his ideas, or perhaps, thought Anna, he was wondering how much he should tell her. 'Your ancestors, the founders of the First Empire, had great powers, cosmic powers. They had discovered how to tap the power of the Web.'

'The Web? What's that?'

'It is everything,' said Tell reverently. 'The power that keeps the atom spinning around its nucleus, the planets around their suns, the suns in the galaxies, the galaxies in the cosmos. We are all part of the Web, everything we do resonates within it, produces vibrations for good or evil.'

'What's all this got to do with the Kaldor?'

'There are power-points in the Web,' said Tell solemnly. 'Energy-junctions where its forces can be tapped, used. The place you call Stonehenge is one of them. We believe the Kaldor discovered some ancient secret hidden there—a source of power they can use for their evil ends.'

'Why? What do they want?'

'You have seen the crew of this ship?' Tell tapped himself on the chest. 'I come from a giant planet, like your Jupiter. The pull of gravity is great—we do not grow very far from the ground! Garm's people live on a world like yours in the Age of Reptiles, a world of jungles and ferocious beasts. Their bodies reverted to the Neanderthal, to give them the strength to survive, but they developed mental powers that more civilised races have forgotten. On Osar's watery planet, life went back to the seas, and the octopoids became the dominant race. Yet here we are, colleagues, friends even. Surely that is as it should be?'

'Well, yes, I suppose so.' Privately Anna doubted if she could ever make friends with a talking octopus, but no doubt the principle was right. 'You mean all intelligent beings are equal, whatever their shape?'

'Not according to the Kaldor,' said Tell grimly. 'They believe the descendants of man are a superior race, born to rule. That rules out Osar's people, and thousands of other intelligent, non-human races. Worse, they say that only those in the true shape of Man are the real elite—which disposes of Garm and myself, and all the other human descendants whose bodies have adapted to the planets they live on. They say that only the Kaldor are the one true race, rulers of the Galaxy by right of birth. By selective breeding, by planned genetic mutation, they have stamped themselves into one mould.' Tell's voice hardened. 'They are cruel, ruthless, utterly without mercy. On the planets they rule all but the Kaldor are abject slaves. By the Power of the Web, I swear to you that they are less human than any of us.' He broke off, seeing Anna's eyes widen with horror. 'I am sorry, my lady, have I frightened you?'

'It isn't that. I was thinking of what you said about the Kaldor—and remembering Kev and Jan are their prisoners.'

5

Prisoners' Bluff

Jan stared at his cousin and rubbed the lump on the back of his aching head. 'Are you telling me we're actually on a UFO—and we're prisoners?'

Kevin waved a hand around the tiny metal cell in which they'd been dumped after the interrogation. 'Well, this isn't a tent on Salisbury Plain, is it? And if you think you're dreaming I'll be glad to give you a pinch.'

'No thanks. I feel bad enough already.' Jan crossed to the cell door and started thumping on it with his fist.

'What do you think you're doing?'

'I'm going to get to see the Captain of this . . . whatever-it-is, and insist he takes us home right away,' said Jan simply.

Kevin stared at him. 'Insist? They were all ready to kill us off just a while ago. They still will, if you start making trouble. Do you want to end up doing a space-walk—without a space suit?'

'Nuts,' said Jan vigorously. 'They wouldn't dare.' He renewed his thumping on the door.

Kevin stared despairingly at his cousin. Somehow he had to make Jan realise how much danger they were in. Jan started kicking at the door, shouting at the top of his voice. 'Hey, out there! Come on, someone answer!'

The door slid back and a Kaldor guard appeared, blaster in hand. 'You have been given food and water.

Why do you cry out? Be silent or you will be executed immediately.'

Jan grabbed the food tray that had been brought in earlier and slung it at the guard's head. It missed by inches and clattered into the corridor. 'I want something decent to eat and drink. And I want to see whoever's in charge here—right away!'

The guard glared at him. He raised his blaster and for a moment it seemed he was about to fire. Kevin stepped in front of him. 'You'd better do as he says. Hurry, or it will be the worse for you!'

The guard backed slowly away, and the door slid closed behind him.

'See?' said Jan, a little uneasily. 'You've got to stand up to these people.'

'Listen,' whispered Kevin fiercely. 'He very nearly killed you just then, and you know it.'

Jan nodded soberly. 'I think you're right. What do we do now?'

'I picked up quite a bit during that explanation. Maybe we can bluff them. Just take your cue from me, okay?'

Before Kevin could explain further, the cell door slid open once more. The two Kaldor officers entered. Guards with blasters stood ready in the corridors behind them.

'What is this?' snapped the leader. 'Your interrogation is now over. You are our prisoners. If you wish to live, be silent and obey.'

Kevin drew a deep breath. 'What is your name?' he said quietly.

The officer stared at him.

'Your name,' repeated Kevin. 'You do know your name? You don't seem to know much else.'

'I am Kiro, commander of this ship. This is Zargon, my First Officer.'

'I am Lord Kevin of Terra, and this is Lord Jan. Our presence on your ship was in the nature of a Test. I regret to inform you that you have failed. You will return us to Earth immediately.'

The two Kaldor were speechless.

Taking advantage of the stunned silence, Kevin launched into his tale. With impressive vagueness he claimed that he and Jan were official Observers, representatives of an all-powerful secret society on Earth, keepers of the strange and mysterious knowledge of the Old Ones. Had the Kaldor been found worthy, they would have been given access to all these incredible secrets. Unfortunately, by their treatment of the Observers they had lost their opportunity. However, if they returned them to Earth at once, he might consider giving them another chance . . .

The Kaldor officers were obviously staggered by the sheer outrageousness of the claim. Kiro said hesitantly, 'What proof . . .'

By now Jan understood his cousin's plan. 'Proof?' he said scornfully. 'We were there waiting for you, weren't we? Who else would know that you were coming?'

'Nobody knew,' said Zargon angrily. 'It was a secret decision of the Kaldor Council. We made landings on Earth, worked out the clues to the ancient knowledge we sought . . .'

'And who left the clues for you to find?' snapped

Jan. 'The secret hidden in Stonehenge is only one of many. Those secrets will be handed on to those who prove worthy . . . not to bullying oafs who confuse violence with intelligence. You may go now.' Jan turned away.

Thunderstruck the Kaldor stared at each other.

Jan ignored them, and the door slid closed. Kevin drew a long shuddering breath and dropped onto the bunk. 'Well, if that didn't impress them, nothing will.'

Jan slapped him on the back encouragingly. 'You were great! Those guys are probably turning the ship round right now.'

There was another long wait. Kevin sat despondently on the bunk, wondering how he could ever have expected such a crazy plan to work. At last the door opened once more. Four Kaldor stood in the metal corridor. They were carrying laser-rifles.

'I guess we overdid it,' said Kevin, unsteadily. 'This looks like the firing squad!'

Jan rose slowly to his feet, tensing himself to spring. If he could just get his hands on one of those rifles . . . Suddenly the Kaldor guards raised their weapons in a curiously formal gesture. To his astonishment he realised it was a kind of salute. A guard said, 'You will follow.' He led the way along the corridor. Jan and Kevin followed, and the other guards fell in behind.

'What's going on?' whispered Kevin. 'Do you think it worked?'

'Beats me. Maybe they're just sending us off in style.'

They reached another door, it slid back and their escort stood aside so they could enter. They found themselves in a small chamber, white-walled and brightly lit. A mirror formed the upper half of one wall, there were recessed basins, and cubicles at the back.

Kevin looked round. 'Doesn't look much like the condemned cell!'

Jan grinned. 'It isn't. I guess our hosts are human after all, Kev. You are now looking at your first interplanetary washroom.' He touched a button and warm soapy water gushed into one of the basins.

Apart from the fact that the water came ready-soaped and the toilets flushed with a violet glow and an alarming whoosh, it was all curiously familiar. When Jan and Kevin finished washing, a sudden blast of hot air blew them dry.

One of the Kaldor came in, indicated a sentry-box-shaped alcove, waving Jan inside. As he stepped into the alcove it lit up. It went dark as he stepped out. There was a whirring, clicking sound. Seconds later a hatch opened at the base of the cubicle and ejected a bundle of clothing—boots, trousers, a close-fitting tunic and a cloak all in gleaming black and silver.

Jan shrugged and began changing into the new clothes. Kevin stepped into the cubicle and it lit up for him, delivering a similar outfit minutes later.

They finished changing and admired themselves in the mirror. The clothes fitted perfectly. They were made of some soft black material. As Kevin stroked his sleeve there was a tiny crackle. (He learned later that the material held a dirt-repelling charge of static electricity, and would never crease or stain.) Kevin felt uncomfortable in this unfamiliar get-up but the black-and-silver uniform suited Jan as if he'd been born to wear it. Despite his youth he was taller and broader than most of the Kaldor and he towered over them impressively. With his yellow-white hair and blue eyes, he might almost have been one of them.

Once they had changed, the waiting Kaldor led them along more corridors and into yet another metal-walled room. This one was larger, with a small central table, and form-fitting chairs. In the central chair sat Kiro, the Kaldor Captain. He rose courteously as they entered. 'I hope you are recovered from your ordeal?'

He was obviously speaking to Jan, but it was Kevin who answered, 'And so you should—considering that you were the cause of it.'

'An unfortunate error on the part of my crew. Those responsible will be punished. Let me offer you some refreshment.' A hatch opened in the table surface and a tray rose into sight. It contained a crystal decanter, silver goblets, and an assortment of dishes containing various strange-looking foods. The Captain poured a purple fluid into the goblets and passed them to Jan and Kevin. 'I think you will find this pleasant. It is brewed from the bell-flowers on my home planet.'

Kevin took a cautious sip. The drink was delicious, fiery and fruity at the same time. He could feel it sending new strength into his body. He looked at Jan. 'Try it, it's okay.'

Jan made no move to taste the drink, setting it down untouched. 'It's going to take more than a free glass of fruit juice to make up for the way we've been treated.'

'I have already made my apologies. We saw you

with those vermin of the League—naturally enough my crew assumed you were with them. Once I had seen you myself, I knew at once that a terrible mistake had been made.'

Kevin smiled coldly, but said nothing. Kiro had been in charge of their interrogation from the beginning. He had ordered that brutal mind-jolt that had slammed a new language into their brains. This sudden change of attitude must mean he believed Kevin's story—or at least, that he wasn't completely sure that the story was false. 'Perhaps the matter can be overlooked,' said Kevin loftily. 'You could not be expected to be aware of our true identity.'

'We should have known there would be an Observer present, but we were not prepared. I only hope that this unfortunate beginning will not prejudice you against us.'

Jan rose. 'We'll see. A lot will depend on how you behave. Now I'm tired.'

Jan got to his feet, nodded curtly at the Kaldor and strode from the room, Kevin close behind him.

A deferential guard was waiting to conduct them to new quarters, a plain metal cabin with two sleeping couches. There a table held a luxurious array of strange food and drinks.

Once they were alone Jan stretched out luxuriously on the couch. 'Well, it worked, Kev! One minute we're in a cell, next it's the VIP suite. You're a genius!'

'Am I?' said Kevin gloomily. 'What do we do now?'

'We keep it up,' said Jan confidently. 'These people are bullies, Kev, and the only thing a bully respects is a bigger bully. So we keep on acting high-and-mighty, and look out for a chance to escape. Don't worry, something will turn up.' Jan yawned. 'Hey, you know something, I really am tired.' He stretched out on the bunk and in a few minutes he was fast asleep.

Kevin looked affectionately at his big cousin, envying him his courage. Nothing seemed to worry Jan for long. He simply couldn't imagine a problem he couldn't deal with somehow or other. And strangely enough, his confidence was often justified. Kevin himself had been ready to surrender to his fate. It was Jan's instinctive defiance that had given him the courage to pull off his bluff. Maybe that was what a hero was, thought Kevin—someone just too brave to do the sensible thing.

Kevin himself was feeling far from heroic. He was suffering from reaction now, his mind full of doubts and fears. He stretched out on the bunk, but his brain was far too active for sleep. What had the Kaldor been after at Stonehenge? Why had they accepted them as 'Observers' with such suspicious speed? And what would they do when they discovered their mistake?

The Kaldor Captain strode arrogantly into the main control room and threw himself into his command chair. The ship was on automatic there was little for anyone to do till they neared their destination. Crewmen moved silently about the room busying themselves with routine checks. He looked up as Zargon came to stand by his side. 'Are our guests settled?'

'Yes, Captain. They are sleeping.'

Kiro nodded thoughtfully. 'It is fortunate that we realised their status in time.'

Zargon frowned. 'Kiro—you are sure . . .'

'Of course I am not sure. But we have always suspected that there were those on Earth who still possessed the Ancient Knowledge. Why else would the League forbid anyone to contact the planet? Those stone circles were set up as a signal. For untold planetary cycles those Old Ones have waited for someone to read the message, to land and make contact. Might they not indeed have Observers present, waiting to see who came?'

'Then why did they not declare themselves?'

'They did—eventually. You heard the insolence with which they spoke to us, the way they demanded treatment befitting their rank. If they were helpless captives, they would be humble and beg for mercy. Since they do not beg for mercy—perhaps they are not merely helpless captives.'

In Kaldor terms the logic was unanswerable. Yet, in spite of everything, Zargon was not convinced.

'If they do have knowledge of the Ancient Wisdom, sooner or later they must reveal it. If they do not, they are no more than useless primitives . . .'

Kiro smiled. 'If that proves to be so, Zargon, then I promise you shall kill them yourself.'

6

Into the Unknown

The control room of the League space ship occupied the whole of the raised dome at the centre of the saucer. It was a huge circular room, and its walls were lined with monitor screens and instrument panels. In the centre of the room was a semicircular control console with three chairs.

The central one was like an enormous throne. On it sat Garm, his big hands making the controls beneath them look like toys. To his right sat Osar, hanging rather than sitting, in a hammock-like device designed to support his round body. The third chair, a kind of bucket seat on a very long pedestal, was obviously Tell's. He hopped nimbly into it and sat beaming at Anna.

Garm looked up. 'Welcome to our conference. Its decisions will affect you. You have a right to speak.'

Anna was taken aback. It hadn't occurred to her that she might actually be consulted about her fate. 'That's very kind of you. It would help me to make my mind up if I knew more about what was going on.'

There was a pause. The three strange beings looked at each other, as if in silent conference. Then Garm said, 'Tell has told you of the history of Old Earth. Many believe that somewhere on your planet, fragments of ancient knowledge still lie hidden.'

'You think that's what the Kaldor were doing at Stonehenge—looking for some ancient secret?'

'Most assuredly,' piped Osar. 'Even now they may have the Secret in their possession. They may be speeding back to Galactic Centre to destroy the League, while we waste time orbiting this barren planet.'

Anna tried to remember the confused events of that night at Stonehenge. 'They were shining some kind of light on one of the monoliths. A pattern appeared, lots of glowing points joined by lines.'

'A star chart,' confirmed Tell. 'Perhaps Stonehenge held not the Secret itself, but the clue to its whereabouts—a clue that could only be followed by a star-travelling race. The Old Ones hoped that someday the new civilisations would rediscover Earth. They left clues for their visitors to find.'

'And this one has been found by the Kaldor,' said Osar bitterly. 'They will use it in their quest to enslave every civilised race in the galaxy.'

'Maybe they haven't found it yet,' said Anna practically. 'If they've got to search a whole planet . . . Why don't we get there before them?'

'Because they have the star chart and we do not,' snapped Osar. 'Unless of course you can reproduce it for us from memory?'

'I only got a glimpse of it. Jan was using his camera all the time though.'

'Unfortunately the Kaldor have your friend Jan as well.'

Tell gave a sudden shout of delight. 'But not his camera! See!'

He took Jan's camera from inside his tunic and

jumped down from his stool. 'I'll take this to the laboratory.'

They waited. Garm stared broodingly ahead, Osar fiddled nervously with the controls making minute and unnecessary adjustments to the ship's orbit.

At last Tell bustled back, rubbing his hands. 'A primitive device, but effective. I have developed the images and transferred them to our vision-circuits.' He touched a control and a picture appeared on the big central vision screen. It showed Anna, on Salisbury Plain, proudly posing against her newly-erected tent.

'Very pretty,' said Osar sardonically. 'But hardly the key to the hidden power of the Old Ones.'

'Wait,' said Tell, and he flashed more pictures onto the screen. There were more shots of the camp, and of Jan and Kevin, clowning about. Anna felt a great wave of anxiety as she saw their grinning faces. What was happening to them now? Were they even alive?

Tell clicked impatiently through the early photographs, then stopped as he reached the one they'd been waiting for—a shot of the League saucer pursuing the Kaldor scout-ship across the night sky. The next shot showed the landed Kaldor ship, Stonehenge looming behind it. There were long shots of the Kaldor studying the megaliths, and then closer shots taken as Jan wriggled nearer.

The last photograph of all was the one they'd been hoping for. It showed three Kaldor grouped round the flattened stone, one shining the torch-like device on it, the other recording the result. The design on the stone showed clearly between the figures of the Kaldor.

'Magnify and stabilise,' rumbled Garm. Tell tuned

the controls, and soon the star-chart swelled until it filled the screen.

'It's a star-system right enough,' said Tell. 'But which? Feed the pattern into the ship's computer, Osar, and check it against the data banks.'

Osar's tentacle snaked out and adjusted controls on the console before him. Symbols began flashing across a read-out screen.

'Positive identification not possible,' piped Osar.

Tell hammered his fist on the console in frustration, and Garm's huge body slumped in dejection.

'Tentative identification follows. Previously unmapped star system, Galactic co-ordinates seven-five-zero-zero-three-nine-six-seven-eight-four. Estimated probability of identification accuracy, fifty-three per cent.'

'Galactic Visual display,' ordered Garm. A huge fiery Catherine wheel of stars filled the central screen.

'At the moment we are still in your solar system,' explained Tell. 'Here.' A pulsating point of light appeared. 'The planet the computer has identified is *here*.' Another light-point appeared—on the other side of the screen. 'As you see, it is on the far side of the Galaxy—a hundred thousand light-years away.'

'Then that's where we're going,' said Anna.

Tell said, 'I do not think you realise what is involved—this vessel is merely a standard cruiser, designed for medium-range travel. To cross the entire Galaxy in a craft this size would be like crossing your widest ocean on a floating log. It could be done only by a colossal jump through hyper-space—a jump of such magnitude that the ship might well disintegrate.'

'If the Kaldor can do it, so can we,' said Anna firmly.

'The whole idea is absurd,' hissed Osar. 'The Kaldor have a specially-built long-range exploration vessel. We don't even know if we have identified the right planet . . .'

'Of course it's the right planet! The people who left the Secret deliberately made it difficult to find.'

'She may be right,' said Garm. 'The planet is on the far side of the Galaxy—surely that must be part of the test.'

'That's right. You want this precious Secret don't you? Well, I want Kevin and Jan back. We shan't get either hanging about in space like a lump of rock!'

Osar was almost twittering in agitation. 'You simply do not realise the danger. The temporal distortion effect alone . . .'

'We could return to Galactic Centre,' said Tell slowly. 'Ask for fresh instructions, transfer to a League Battle Cruiser.'

'While the Kaldor ransack the planet for the Secret!' Garm shook his head. 'The girl is right. We shall set off at once.' He turned to Anna. 'First we shall take you back to Earth . . .'

'Oh no you don't! Kevin and Jan are still missing. I'd be wondering what had happened to them for the rest of my life. Besides you haven't got time. The Kaldor had the star-chart before you, remember. They'll be well on their way by now.'

There was a momentary silence. Osar and Tell were looking at Garm. For all the easy informality of their behaviour, it was clear that the huge Neanderthal was the real leader.

At last Garm said, 'You have the true spirit of Old Earth. We shall do as you say. Tell, run up the boosters to maximum power. Forget the safety margins. Osar, compute the hyper-jump co-ordinates.'

Anna sat back and watched their preparations. Now the decision was taken she could only keep out of the way. Under Tell's hands the drive motors produced a steadily deeper thrumming that shook the control room. Osar sat hunched over his computer, tentacles flickering wildly over the controls, his huge eyes absorbing the never-ending flow of symbols on the read-out screen.

Following Garm's instructions, Anna lay back on her seat, which extended and moulded itself into a couch. Finally Osar hissed, 'Now!', and Garm's huge hand dragged back a master-switch.

Anna felt a horrible wrenching distortion, like being turned inside-out. The control-room seemed to break up and swirl around her. For a moment she felt the ship really had blown up and she was drifting with its debris in space.

Gradually everything stabilised. She was back in the control-room on her couch. The others sat braced in their chairs.

Anna's voice came out in a dry croak. 'What happened?' she whispered. 'Where are we?'

It was Tell who answered her. 'That was the Jump. Now we are nowhere—nowhere and no-when.' He pointed to the screen. The swirl of stars had vanished, replaced by a swirling grey nothingness. 'We are in the void. When Osar computes re-entry we shall emerge. Perhaps into the heart of a sun, perhaps in a black hole, perhaps, if we are very lucky, somewhere close to our destination—on the far side of the Galaxy. Our quest has begun!'

7

Across the Galaxy

It was a dead planet swinging in orbit around a dying sun. Once it had been an important border-world, marking the outer limits of the long-vanished Empire. One great city covered much of the planet's surface, its towers of metal jutting high into the air.

Long ago its streets and walk-ways had been thronged with Imperial Guards, defending the frontier against attack from the barbarian worlds, with explorers, prospectors, administrators. Now all were gone. The City stood empty, half in ruins, inhabited only by the creatures that came in from the wilderness beyond, a wilderness that year by year encroached upon the City more and more. City and Jungle were locked in silent struggle, a death-grapple that would end only when the planet itself was dead.

As the Kaldor scout ship dropped down towards the planet, Jan and Kevin studied the approaching surface on the vision screen. It was an impressive sight, great towers of metal, some half-ruined, projecting through a swirling curtain of mist.

'The air of the planet is thin, but breathable,' said Kiro. 'Some discomfort may be felt if a long journey is necessary.' He looked pointedly at Kevin and Jan.

These knew at once what the Kaldor meant. They had arrived at their destination. Now it was time for them to prove their claims. Since Kevin had no idea what they were seeking, let alone where it was, that was going to be difficult. He tried to maintain his bluff. 'We're only here to observe. It is for you to prove your worth by reaching your goal unaided.'

'Time and resources are limited,' said Zargon pointedly. 'We cannot search an entire planet. If we attempt it, we shall all die here.' His expression made it clear who would be the first to go.

Inspiration flashed suddenly across Kevin's mind. 'Exactly what is it that you seek?'

'We seek—' began Kiro.

Zargon interrupted him. 'Who should know better than an Observer?'

Foiled again, thought Kevin. Let's try it another way. He gave the two Kaldor a look of bored contempt. 'I'm not talking about its form, I mean its true nature.'

Kiro said hesitantly, 'We seek power . . .'

'Exactly. And power is energy, is it not?'

Kiro rounded angrily on his subordinate. 'As soon as we land, set sensors on maximum range and probe for any unusual energy source on the planet.'

Jan drew Kevin aside. 'Look, Kev, what do you think you're playing at? We don't know what they're after, or where it is—do we?'

'As long as they don't know we don't know—we're all right. The minute they find out the truth—we're dead.'

'How long can we keep it up?'

'Not much longer. Kiro's getting more and more suspicious—and Zargon never really believed us in the first place.'

'So what do we do?'

Kevin grinned. 'We improvise!'

Jan whispered ruefully, 'I think you're actually enjoying this!'

Kevin saw the two Kaldor officers watching their conference from the other side of the control room. 'Shut up and look haughty,' he hissed, and returned to his study of the vision screen.

As the planetary surface rushed closer and closer, Kevin realised that his cousin's words were true. Despite the dangers, he was enjoying this game of bluff and counter-bluff. There was a fierce excitement in matching wits with his alien enemies.

Obviously Jan felt differently about things. His cousin preferred the kind of danger you could charge head-on, an enemy he could flatten with a few solid punches. Well, he'd just have to realise there was a place for brains as well as brawn.

The metal towers on the screen hurtled towards them, until their walls filled the screen. There was the faintest of vibrations and the screen went blank.

'Landing procedure completed,' reported Zargon.

'Maintain emergency take-off readiness. Commence energy-scan,' ordered Kiro.

Crew members busied themselves at the instrument consoles. A low beeping sound began ringing through the control room. Kevin watched a crewman operate a wheel-shaped control, presumably rotating the scanner beam around the ship. Suddenly the beeping increased its frequency. The crewman looked up. 'Powerful energy-source located, sir. Bearing one-four-zero.'

'Range?'

'Too close for an accurate reading. The source is so powerful it's affecting the instruments.'

With a sigh of relief, Kevin realised that his gamble seemed to have paid off. Unfortunately, it had paid off for the Kaldor as well.

Kiro's eyes were gleaming with excitement. 'We shall leave at once. Bring the portable energy scanner, and one squad of guards.'

Zargon looked at Jan and Kevin. 'And our two Observers?'

'They will be coming with us—in case we need the benefits of their advice.'

From behind the shattered plasti-glass window of one of the towers, bright eyes were watching the terrifying object that had suddenly appeared in the square. Whatever it was, it was new—and newness meant danger.

From their hiding-place the watchers saw a door open in the ship and a ramp slide out. Black-clad figures emerged, descended the ramp, and stood waiting. The watching creatures reached nervously for their weapons . . .

Shivering in the chill dank air, Kevin wrapped himself in his cloak. Despite the dangers of his situation, his mind was full of a sense of wonder. He was standing on the soil of another world. Or to be strictly accurate on its cracked and rubble-littered paving stones. He had crossed the Galaxy.

The ship had landed in the centre of an enormous circular space, ringed in with jagged black metal towers. In the centre was a huge pool with a fountain-like structure in the middle. But the fountain was silent now, and the stagnant water of the pool was covered with weeds. Coarse spiky grass had forced its way up through the paving stones and many of the surrounding towers were overgrown with vines. At intervals narrow black-surfaced roads led off from the plaza, disappearing into the distance.

Jan pointed. 'Look how narrow those streets are. They must have had quite a traffic problem.'

'Maybe they didn't have traffic at all. Look!'

The streets were bordered with narrow metal paths, rows of them one above the other, stretching upwards in tiers. 'Walkways,' said Kevin. 'Step out of your front door and ride to wherever you want to go.'

'Why so many?'

Kevin considered. 'Probably the lower ones were for local journeys, and the ones above for longer trips. The very top ones probably ran to different cities altogether.'

'Must have been quite some civilisation. Where did everybody go?'

Kiro appeared. He held a small black box in his hands, with a compass-like dial set into the lid, and control-buttons in the side. He switched the device on, and the needle quivered into life. It spun wildly for a moment, then steadied, pointing straight down the road to the left.

Suddenly one of the guards raised his rifle and raked the face of the nearest tower with the purple glow of the laser beam. A whole row of windows burst into crystal fragments, and drips of molten metal ran down the face of the building. The guard lowered the weapon. 'Someone was watching us.'

Zargon surveyed the charred and smoking ruin that was the front of the building. 'No doubt you have disposed of them. Shall we be on our way, Commander?'

Kiro nodded, and the little group set off. As they moved along the narrow streets that ran between the towers, Kevin's face was grim. The little incident had pushed him to a decision—one that could easily cost them their lives.

Only one of the creatures in the building survived the searing blast of the laser-beam. Terrified it limped along echoing corridors and through deserted halls, clutching a charred patch of fur on its leg. It came to a shattered window, sprang through the open space, and swung nimbly away through the vines that festooned the building. One thought filled its terrified mind. The gods had returned at last. But they had not brought the wonderful gifts that had been promised. The gods were angry, wreaking death and destruction. The creature collapsed gasping on a branch, husbanding its strength for the long and dangerous journey that lay ahead. The Tribe must be warned . . .

In the blackness of deep space the League's flying saucer flickered into existence. Anna clutched the edges of her couch. Coming out of hyper-space was almost as bad as going in. She became aware of a low murmur of voices.

Garm, Tell and Osar were studying the star pattern on the vision screen. 'We are here,' piped Osar triumphantly. 'We have crossed the Galaxy in a single jump, and reached the star system we seek. Truly I am unrivalled amongst star navigators!'

'We have reached *a* star system,' said Garm. 'Tell, check against the chart.'

Anna saw a second star pattern appear on the screen —the chart they had taken from Jan's camera. The two pictures blurred for a moment, and then merged. Tell gave a rasping sigh of relief. 'Osar, you are almost as brilliant as you think you are!'

Anna sat up. 'Well, so we're here. Now what?'

'We have reached the star system, but not yet the planet itself,' said Garm. 'Now we must travel on in normal space. How long, Tell?'

Tell studied the instruments in front of him. 'Perhaps two decads, not longer.'

A decad, Anna had learned, was one tenth of the arbitrary ship's day, which was about ten hours long. 'What do we do when we reach the planet? There's a whole world to search, and we don't even know what we are looking for.'

'We are looking for Kaldor,' said Garm. 'Once we have found them, the Secret will not be far away.'

'Nor will your friends,' added Tell. 'If the Kaldor have made them prisoner, we may be able to release them.'

'How will you find the Kaldor?'

'It will not be easy,' admitted Tell. 'If we are lucky we may be able to pick up the energy-field of their ship.'

'Suppose it has already landed?'

'There will still be an energy-trace—but it will be very small.'

'And what will you do when you find them?'

'We shall ask them to release your friends,' said Garm. 'And we shall attempt to persuade them that the knowledge they seek must be passed over to the League, and used for the good of all the galaxy.'

'Ask? Persuade?' said Anna scornfully. 'You'll have to do more than that. Last time you met they started shooting on sight.'

Garm's deep voice was solemn. 'It is a serious thing to take the life of any living being. But if there is no other way, then we shall destroy them. Infinite is the Web.'

Softly, Tell made the ritual response. 'May its power protect us.'

They were resting in one of the open squares very like the one in which they had first landed. Indeed the whole City seemed to be laid out on absolutely regular lines. Towers, roads and walkways, a square with a fountain or some huge piece of abstract sculpture, more streets and walkways, another square . . . everything on an enormous scale.

Jan and Kevin sat on the low stone wall that surrounded the pool, eating rations handed out by one of the Kaldor. Tasteless distilled water in a plastic flask, grey cubes of food concentrate . . . No-one could accuse the Kaldor of being gourmets, thought Kevin. It was only one of the many things he disliked about them. The two Kaldor officers stood some way away, studying the energy-tracking device.

Kevin edged closer to his cousin and whispered, 'Jan, listen. It's time we decided on a plan.'

'I thought we had a plan—staying alive.'

'We know the Kaldor are after some great Secret, right? Something that will give them tremendous power . . .'

'So?'

'So we've got to stop them from getting it.'

'*Us?* Why?'

'Because they're ruthless killers, they're out to take over the Galaxy . . .'

'Are you crazy?' whispered Jan. 'Look, we got mixed up in a war—but that doesn't mean we've got to join in.'

'The Kaldor were going to toss us out in space, remember, until we managed to bluff them. They'll kill us anyway, as soon as they get what they're after.'

'So what do you want us to do?'

'Escape,' said Kevin calmly. 'Find what they're after, and get hold ot it before them. Then we can do some kind of deal. Better still, we can make contact with the other side, the League, and do a deal with them.'

'What makes you so sure they're any better than the Kaldor?'

Kevin grinned. 'I'm not—but any enemy of the Kaldor is a friend of mine! Anyway, keep your eyes open. When we get a chance we'll make a run for it.'

Suddenly they heard raised voices. Kiro and Zargon seemed to be having some kind of dispute. 'We cannot march through this desolation indefinitely,' Kiro said angrily. 'We must return to the ship and attempt to land closer to our goal.'

'With respect, Commander, the energy detector cannot be used while the ship is in flight. The signal is clear and strong now—we must be very close.'

'The further from the ship, the greater our danger. We know this planet still holds some kind of life. What if we are attacked?'

'Here?' said Zargon scornfully. 'What could harm us here? Some primitive life-forms may have survived—but if they attack us we shall know how to deal with them.' He nodded towards the guards with their laser-rifles.

Something flashed silently across the square and a guard staggered back choking, an arrow in his throat.

8

The Monster in the Pool

For a second everyone was frozen with sheer astonishment. As more arrows zipped across the square, Kaldor guards began firing in the direction of the attack, Kiro snatched the hand-blaster from his belt, Zargon ran to snatch the laser-rifle from the fallen guard. The Kaldor were reacting to danger with impressive speed, though several more guards dropped with arrows in them before the rest of the squad found cover.

Jan and Kevin ducked down behind the parapet. The arrows were coming from the corner tower, a vine-festooned ruin with rows of shattered windows. The Kaldor guards were pouring laser-bolt after laser-bolt into the buildings. The lurid purple flare of the laser-beams filled the square, and there was a red glow from inside the tower as the building caught fire.

Kevin jabbed his cousin in the ribs. 'Now's our chance.' Zargon had put the energy-detector down on the parapet so he could use the rifle. 'We can pinch that gadget and find the Secret before them.'

Before Jan could reply, Kevin sprinted along the parapet, snatched up the energy-detector and dashed down one of the narrow streets leading away from the square.

Choices flashed through Jan's mind at the speed of light. Follow Kevin? Zargon had seen Kevin flash by him and was already swinging round, bringing the laser-rifle to bear on the fleeing figure. And Kevin was running down a long narrow passage with nowhere to hide . . .

Jan realised he had only one chance of survival. He ran up to Zargon and snatched the laser-rifle from his grip, giving the Kaldor a shove that sent him staggering. Fumbling for the firing stud, Jan swung the weapon round to cover Kevin, who was looking over his shoulder to see if his cousin was following. 'Come on,' yelled Kevin—and Jan fired. Just above Kevin's head, a chunk of building exploded in flame. With a burst of speed, Kevin shot round a corner and disappeared from sight.

By now Kiro had realised what was happening. 'After him,' he screamed. The nearest guard set off in pursuit. To follow Kevin he had to cross open ground and the unseen enemies were ready. Three arrows thudded into the guard's body at once, and he fell twitching to the ground.

Zargon was on his feet now, face twisted with rage, fumbling for the blaster in his belt. Before he could draw the weapon, Jan threw him the laser-cannon with a force that sent him staggering back.

'It is too late. You have let him escape.'

Kiro was staring at them in astonishment. 'What is happening here?'

'My colleague tried to persuade me to join him in stealing the Secret.'

Kiro looked hard at him. 'And you refused?'

'You saw for yourself. When Zargon's negligence gave him his chance, I tried to kill him myself.'

By now Zargon had the laser-rifle trained on Jan.

'You lie. *You* let him escape. Soon he will be found and destroyed—but you will die now.'

'You are a fool, Zargon,' said Jan wearily. 'If I wanted to betray you, I would have escaped with him.' Turning his back on the weapon, he swung round to Kiro. 'You have another energy-detector of course?'

'It is in the ship.'

Jan gave the weary sign of superior intelligence faced with perpetual stupidity. 'In the ship, of course. May I suggest we return and fetch it?'

'Do not listen to him,' shrieked Zargon. 'He seeks only to save his friend.'

'When my colleague is recaptured, I shall execute him myself,' said Jan calmly. 'But without another energy-detector we shall not succeed in finding either him *or* the Secret. Thanks to you he now has a considerable start. Our only chance is to find the traitor and Secret together.'

Kiro hesitated. The contrast between Zargon's gibbering anger and Jan's calm certainty was having effect. 'We shall do as the Observer suggests. Zargon, you were negligent to bring only one energy-detector. Order the men to fall back.'

Zargon rapped an order to the guards. The tower holding their attackers was well ablaze now, sending a great plume of black smoke into the grey sky. No more arrows came from it. The enemy had been forced to retreat.

Jan looked at the burning tower. 'We can use this as a marker, return to this point by ship, and take up the search again.'

Kiro nodded reluctantly. 'An excellent idea, Observer. It will save a good deal of time. I shall make sure that our next expedition is better prepared.' He strode back the way they had come, Jan at his side.

Still carrying the laser-rifle, Zargon followed with the surviving guards. As he followed Jan's tall figure with his eyes, his fingers caressed the firing-stud of the weapon . . .

Kevin sped on through the silent grey streets, the sounds of battle fading away behind him. He ran and ran until he was gasping for breath in the thin cold air. Then too tired to run further he took shelter in an ornately decorated doorway, and tried to collect his thoughts. He'd made his impulsive dash on sheer instinct, an overpowering feeling that he had to get away from the Kaldor, and that this was the time. He'd assumed his cousin would follow, and he still hadn't recovered from the shock of seeing that, far from joining in his escape, Jan had apparently done his best to blow his head off.

Surely Jan hadn't really changed sides? On Earth Kevin would have trusted him completely. But they weren't on Earth. In this world everything was strange and different. Perhaps Jan was different too. Certainly there was a ruthlessly practical streak in Jan. If instinct told him that killing Kevin was the only way to survive . . .

Kevin decided to forget Jan for the moment and concentrate on more immediate problems. If he was to find the Secret before the Kaldor and somehow turn it against them, he'd better be on his way. The loss of the detector would not delay the Kaldor for long. Kevin looked down at the little box. Its needle was still pointing firmly onto the mysterious energy-source. Using the detector as his compass, he resumed his journey.

Anna sat with her eyes fixed on the vision screen, while the surface of the planet flowed endlessly below her. It seemed to consist of one enormous city—towers, streets, squares, the same pattern repeated over and over again, everything completely regular, and everything utterly deserted.

Anna kept hoping she would be the one to spot the Kaldor ship. Perhaps she would even see Jan or Kevin walking along those silent grey streets. It was ridiculous, she knew. At this height they would appear on the screen as no more than moving dots. The only real hope of finding them lay with Osar, who sat hunched over his delicate detector-instruments, his huge golden eyes alert for any flicker of the dials.

Anna turned to him. 'Have you found anything?'

'There is nothing,' said Osar despondently. 'Not a trace. Unless we find them soon, we must abandon the search.'

'No, you can't! You can't just leave them.'

Tell and Garm were looking on sympathetically. 'It is not a question of choice,' said Garm. 'Unless we leave this planet soon, we shall not be able to leave at all.'

'Our energy-resources are limited,' explained Tell. 'They are already strained by the huge jump across the Galaxy. Unless we husband them carefully, we shall not be able to return to Galactic Centre.'

'But you won't give up yet?' pleaded Anna.

'No,' said Garm reassuringly. 'We shall not give up yet. While a single erg of energy remains, we shall continue the search.'

The Kaldor force was weary and discouraged by the time they reached the ship, returning not as they'd hoped, with the treasure in their grasp, but instead tired and defeated, with most of their number dead. Jan noticed that no attempt had been made to bring back the slain, or even to give them any kind of burial. The bodies had simply been left where they had fallen. Now, back in the ship, they were finishing a hasty meal of the usual food-concentrates before setting off again.

Zargon rose. 'I will prepare the new crew members, Commander. We lost six, did we not?'

'Replace them, and add three more,' ordered Kiro. 'We must expect another attack. Issue them with laser-rifles.'

'How many crew have you got on this ship?' asked Jan curiously.

Zargon smiled, 'As many as we need. Come, Earthman, I will show you.'

He led Jan through the metal corridors of the ship, and down to a circular chamber on the lower levels. Most of the chamber was taken up by a transparent coffin-shaped tank which gave off a dim, greenish glow. It seemed to be filled with a murky liquid, rather like pea soup.

Zargon went to an instrument-panel, and stabbed rapidly at the controls. There was a hum of power, and the glow from the tank brightened into a fierce green blaze. The viscous liquid began to swirl and eddy, and a shape started to form. Slowly it solidified, broke the surface of the liquid and rose to its feet. It was the figure of a man, or rather a Kaldor, with the same fair hair, blue eyes and wiry build of all the others. It might have been Zargon's twin—or Kiro's for that matter.

As the figure stepped from the tank, a blast of warm air swept the room, drying off the traces of liquid. Zargon gave a nod of satisfaction, and re-programmed the controls. More liquid glugged into the tank. It swirled and eddied, and another shape began to form . . .

The eerie process was repeated again and again, until nine identical figures stood waiting, ranked in three rows of three. Zargon turned challengingly to Jan. 'You see, Earthman?'

'Very impressive,' said Jan dryly. 'The rest of the family, I suppose?'

'They are clones. Identical replicas of myself, each one grown in the nutrient fluid from a single cell of my body.'

'Why go to the trouble? There *are* easier ways of producing people.'

Zargon looked surprised. 'But these are *true* Kaldor. The elite of our planet as I am myself. It is not easy, even for us, to breed completely true. Height, build, colouring, mental capacity, all are exactly laid down by the Tyrant of Kaldor himself. Once a true specimen has been obtained, it can be reproduced by cloning, as many times as needed.'

Jan was impressed, though he tried not to let it show. 'How many can you produce?'

'Here on the ship? No more than a few hundred,

the nutrient supply is limited. In the great cloning tanks on the home planet—millions upon millions! Enough to put an army of occupation on every habitable planet in the Galaxy.'

Jan envisaged a fleet of Kaldor ships landing on Earth, each one disgorging an endless army of black-clad soldiers.

He looked at the motionless figures. 'Don't seem any too lively, do they?'

Zargon shrugged. 'There is an initial period of disorientation. They will be clothed, fed, armed, briefed. Then they will be Kaldor warriors.'

'Like the others on this ship . . . . Now that I think of it, they're none too lively either, are they? Only you and Kiro seem to talk, think, give orders.'

'The cloning process has limitations,' admitted Zargon reluctantly. 'Certain personality elements are only faintly present. But Kaldor scientists are at work improving the process.'

'But until the guys back in the lab get it right, you're stuck with zombies? Cannon-fodder, who can follow simple orders, and die when they're told to!'

Zargon said coldly, 'What else need a soldier do?'

Jan turned away. 'Well, you'd better get your toy soldiers kitted out, Zargon. They've got work to do.'

Kevin rounded the base of yet another tower—and found himself looking at a Palace.

It lay on the far side of an enormous square, and it was circled by a moat. It seemed to be made of some kind of crystal, and its towers, battlements and turrets shone like a beacon in the surrounding gloom.

Kevin checked the energy-detector. Its needle was pointing straight towards the Palace, quivering with eager life. The object of his quest must be very close.

Kevin crossed the square and stood gazing thoughtfully into the stagnant weed-covered water of the moat. There was no sign of a bridge. He could swim across of course—it wasn't much more than about three lengths of a swimming pool. But there was something very unattractive about the murky water. Kevin decided to look for some other solution.

He wandered along the edge of the moat, the Palace of crystal gleaming tantalizingly on the other side. The needle on the energy-indicator was still pointing unerringly towards it. He came to a kind of wharf, a scattering of low buildings and a landing stage. There were no boats, but stacked against the side of one of the buildings was a pile of huge metal containers. Kevin lifted one. It was about twice his own length, and felt light and strong at the same time. He carried it down to the moat and pushed it in. It floated placidly on the still water.

Kevin looked round. He found a plank-shaped strip of metal alloy leaning against a building. He climbed into the tank, sat cross-legged in the centre, and began paddling with the metal strip. The tank shot away from the bank, and began spinning like a top.

Its lightness made it unstable, like a coracle, but eventually Kevin mastered the knack of steering, and began a slow progress across the moat. Talk about going to sea in a sieve . . .

He was about half-way across when he saw the ripple following him. Something was moving beneath the surface. Judging by the size of the ripple it was something large . . .

Too late to turn back now . . . Kevin paddled slowly on. The ripple came after him. Soon he was two-thirds of the way across and had just about convinced himself the ripple was some harmless trick of the current.

A huge fanged head shot straight up out of the water and lunged hungrily towards him.

9

Palace of Peril

Kevin saw a blunt, flattish head on the end of a long sinewy neck, several rows of gleaming teeth, and two tiny red eyes. Weed and water streamed from the creature's head as it broke the surface.

He didn't hang around long enough to make a more detailed study. The moment the horror appeared Kevin jumped out of his improvised boat and made for the bank at his best Australian Crawl.

The shining metal container saved his life. Missing Kevin by inches, the monster lunged for it, clamping down on the container with those rows of gleaming teeth. The metal buckled like silver paper, and the tank was soon a chunk of chewed wreckage in the creature's mouth. It chomped on the metal for a while, decided it wasn't good to eat, tossed it aside with an angry roar. By now Kevin was climbing out onto the far bank. The movement caught the monster's eye, and it set off after him.

Kevin sprinted through an enormous crystal arch in the wall surrounding the Palace. He found himself in a huge courtyard. On the other side was a door, presumably giving entrance to the Palace. Kevin turned for a better look at the monster, assuming that now he was on land he was relatively safe. The assumption was wrong. The monster, it seemed, was more of a giant lizard than a snake. It had clambered out of the moat on a set of thick, clawed legs and was heading for the crystal archway like an express-train entering a tunnel. The arch wasn't quite big enough, and half-way through the monster stuck fast, with a bellow of anger.

Kevin turned and hared across the courtyard, hoping the beast would stay jammed long enough for him to get into the Palace. Gasping he hurried towards the doorway—then all at once it looked as if he wasn't to get inside the Palace so easily after all.

A towering metal shape glided forward, barring his path. It was an enormous robot.

Kevin skidded to an astonished halt. The robot had a cylindrical metal body with a metal sphere on top to form the head. A huge circular lens gleamed in the centre of the sphere, giving it the air of a metal Cyclops. It had flexible arms, and glided on a cylindrical metal base, presumably moving on some kind of hovercraft principle. The thing was at least three times Kevin's height, and it towered above him, completely blocking the door. 'HALT!' it commanded in a booming voice. 'YOU ARE NOW ENTERING A HIGH SECURITY ZONE. PLEASE PRODUCE YOUR PASS AND HOLD IT BEFORE MY SCANNER.'

Kevin glanced over his shoulder. The lizard-monster wrenched itself free, wrecking the arch in the process, and began thundering across the courtyard. Giant monsters, giant robots, thought Kevin resentfully. Why did everything on this planet have to be so *big?* Looking up at the robot Kevin pointed to the approaching monster. 'Never mind me,' he shouted. 'Why don't you ask that thing for its pass?'

He jumped to one side as the monster came hurtling forward. It reared back in astonishment as it saw the robot. To Kevin's amazement, the robot followed his suggestion.

'HALT!' it said again. 'YOU ARE NOW ENTERING A HIGH SECURITY ZONE. PLEASE PRODUCE YOUR PASS AND HOLD IT BEFORE MY SCANNER.'

Apparently the monster didn't have a pass either. It lunged at the robot, slamming into it with its blunt fanged head, almost knocking it from its base with the force of its charge. 'DESIST!' said the robot sternly. 'YOU ARE INTERFERING WITH MY FUNCTION I SHALL REPORT YOUR ACTION TO CENTRAL CONTROL. YOU ARE LIABLE TO A FINE OF UP TO ONE HUNDRED GALACTIC CREDITS.'

Unimpressed by this threat at the lizard-monster lunged at the robot again, the savage claws making deep scratches in the shining metal.

'I AM AUTHORISED TO RESIST ILLEGAL ACTIONS WITH PUNITIVE MEASURES,' boomed the robot sternly. 'PRODUCE YOUR PASS IMMEDIATELY, OR LEAVE THE AREA. THIS IS YOUR FINAL WARNING.'

The monster responded with a roar of anger and clamped its teeth on one metal arm. A shutter slid back in the robot's barrel-like chest and a small nozzle appeared. There was a faint crackle, and the purple glare of a laser ray. The ray was fitful and erratic, but it was enough to discourage the monster. It gave a scream of pain, whipped round and slithered rapidly across the yard, through the ruined archway, and back into the moat with a colossal splash.

Kevin dodged past the security robot and ran into the Palace. He heard the robot's voice boom out behind him. 'YOU ARE ADVISED TO REPORT TO THE MAIN SECURITY OFFICE AND OBTAIN A DULY AUTHORISED PASS.' He wondered if the monster would take any notice.

When he was far enough from the entrance to feel safe, Kevin paused to look about him. He was in an enormously wide corridor which stretched ahead as far as he could see, curving out of sight in the far distance. Once again Kevin was struck by the sheer size of everything on this planet. The corridor was high as well as broad, its ceiling lost in shadows. Dimly glowing light-globes were set at intervals along the walls. The corridor was carpeted in some soft iridescent material that glowed with subtly changing colours. Kevin had a twinge of guilt about dripping muddy water on the Royal carpet. He looked down at his clothes and found them perfectly dry and clean—somehow the material had just shaken off the water. Another point for Kaldor technology, he thought—which reminded him about the energy-detector inside his tunic. He took it out and looked at it. The needle was pointing to the right. He needed to find a side corridor of some kind . . . Kevin hurried on.

At intervals doorways led off from the corridor. Kevin stopped now and again to look inside the rooms to which they led. All the chambers were enormous, their vast interiors concealed in shadowy gloom. Some looked like state rooms or conference chambers, others might have been living rooms or sleeping quarters, but all were built on the same colossal scale.

At last Kevin reached a right-hand corridor junction. He turned the corner and found himself facing another robot. Kevin groaned, wondering if there would be another demand for his pass. This robot was smaller than the first, though of the same basic shape, and it was moving to and fro as if on sentry duty. As he got closer he saw the robot had a plastic sack attached to the back of its body-case, and a suction nozzle on a long, flexible arm projecting from its front. It was vacuum-cleaning the carpet.

When Kevin came up to it the little robot drew respectfully to one side, waiting for him to pass. Once he'd turned the corner it resumed its task. Kevin went on, shaking his head in astonishment. Rampaging monsters on the outside, robot housemaids on the inside . . .

The inner corridor along which he was now walking was both narrower and darker than the first, and there were no doors leading off. Far in the distance was a faint green glow, like the point of light at the end of a long tunnel. Kevin marched on and on feeling mentally and physically exhausted. It was like walking up a down escalator—you had no feeling of getting anywhere. He plodded forward and at last he reached the source of the glow. A massive door blocked off the end of the corridor. It was made of some translucent material, and it glowed green in the semi-darkness. Kevin checked the energy-indicator. Whatever he was looking for was somewhere on the other side of that door.

He gave the door a tentative push, and it swung smoothly open. He went through and the door closed silently behind him. Kevin stood staring about him in sheer astonishment.

He was in a jungle.

Tell leaned forward, pointing eagerly at the viewing screen. 'There—we have found them!'

They had been gliding high above the City for what seemed like a very long time, the League ship silent and invisible behind its protective screens. Now, at last, they had found what they were looking for—the black Kaldor scout-ship was standing in one of the City squares. Even as they watched, the Kaldor ship took off.

'Maybe we're too late,' said Anna in alarm. 'Maybe they've found what they're after and are already on the way home.'

'Watch,' said Garm.

From their superior height they saw the Kaldor ship rise a few hundred feet in the air, fly parallel with the ground for a short distance, then land in another square identical to the first.

'Go lower,' ordered Garm. 'But stay out of range of their detector-beams.'

'If we move too close they will find us, even through the shields,' grumbled Osar. His tentacles moved obediently over the controls, and the League ship descended to hover silent and invisible high above the square.

The scout ship's landing ramp emerged, and three Kaldor appeared. They stood looking around them—studying the dials of an instrument that one of them was carrying. They had a brief conference amongst themselves, then orders were given, more Kaldor appeared from the ship, and eventually about a dozen set off, marching away from the square.

At the head of the marching group was a tall, broad-shouldered figure. He wore the same black and silver uniform as the others, but there was something familiar about him . . .

Anna leaned forward. 'Can you manage a close-up of that one in front?'

Osar zoomed in on the tall figure until his head and shoulders filled the screen. He had the same blond hair and regular features as the other Kaldor, and his cold blue eyes stared arrogantly around him.

'It's Jan!' gasped Anna. 'That one in front—it's my cousin Jan!'

Tell said consolingly, 'He may have been forced to join them . . . Can you see your other friend?'

Osar pulled back the video beam and Anna scanned the marching group. 'No, there's no sign of him. Maybe he's still a prisoner in the ship.'

Was that what had happened, Anna wondered. Had Jan joined up with the Kaldor? And what about Kevin? There was a powerful streak of obstinacy in her small cousin. If he'd refused to join the Kaldor, then perhaps he was already dead. She saw the concern in the faces of the three others. 'Well, what do we do now?'

'We follow,' said Osar.

Garm shook his head. 'We must do better than that. We must reach their destination before them. Osar, plot them onto an aerial map of the City.'

The picture of the marching Kaldor was replaced by a map. It showed the square, the scout ship, and the network of streets around. The Kaldor appeared as a little group of dots, moving slowly away from the ship.

'Pull back still further—and project their line of movement.'

Osar obeyed. A line appeared on the map-screen, beginning at the square where they'd first seen the Kaldor, creeping slowly forward to the second square where the ship had landed, moving on to join the group of dots, and then going on beyond them. The line went on and on until it reached an enormous circular pattern at the far edge of the map. 'There,' said Garm softly.

Anna looked at the huge circular shape. 'What is it?'

'Their destination,' said Garm softly. 'We shall reach it before them.'

The League cruiser rose higher and glided over the City.

Giant trees with enormous knotted trunks rose so high that they hid the sky. A hidden sun beat down with tremendous force. Vines and plants and creepers of every kind struggled up towards the light swarming over the twisted knotted tree-trunks in rich profusion. Shrubs and bushes and thorn-trees were everywhere. For a moment Kevin stood in total confusion, his bearings completely lost. He tried to work out where he was. Judging by its frontage the Palace was enormous. Had he managed to cross it completely, and emerge on the other side? Suddenly Kevin realised the truth.

He remembered the vast curved frontage of the building, reflected in the curve of that first corridor. The Palace was built in the shape of a wheel. The outer corridor was the rim, the narrower one he'd just come down one of the spokes. Incredible as it seemed this jungle was at the hub, actually inside the Palace itself.

Kevin stared up at the fierce yellow light that beat down through the dense screen of tropical vegetation, and breathed the warm humid air. He remembered the dull grey skies of the planet's surface. This blazing sun above him was artificial. The whole place was artificial, a colossal greenhouse as big as one of the jungles of Earth.

Perhaps the rulers of this planet had built the jungle as a place where they could escape from the chill dank air of their dying planet, feel the warmth of sunshine again, see the fresh green of tropical plants, the bright colours of the flowers. Now, abandoned for untold thousands of years, the pleasure ground had reverted to jungle, while the artificial sun still beat down from the clear blue sky.

Still, artificial or not, the jungle had to be crossed. The energy-sensor pointed firmly towards its centre. Wishing he had an elephant gun and a line of native porters, Kevin began forcing his way through the jungle.

It wasn't an easy journey. There were faint traces of a path, but it was almost completely overgrown. There were sinister rustlings in the jungle around him, and from time to time a fierce cawing from the tree-tops above.

It occurred to Kevin that this jungle might be inhabited, by animals, perhaps even by intelligent life. He was just wondering what those inhabitants might be like when something landed on top of him. It was a net of some kind, woven from vines and creepers. Kevin struggled desperately to free himself, but the folds of the net entangled his limbs and bore him down. Grey-furred shapes dropped chattering from the trees, long yellow fangs glinting in black-muzzled faces. They gathered up the net between them, wrapping it more firmly around their prisoner. To his horror Kevin felt himself beginning to rise up in the air. Higher and higher went the net with its struggling burden, until the jungle floor was a dizzying distance below. In a series of swooping rushes the grey-furred creatures carried their captive clear up to the leafy jungle roof.

10

The Warriors of Arko

Protected by its invisibility-screen the League cruiser hovered high above the Palace. On the vision-screen Anna could see the line of marching Kaldor heading straight for the edge of the moat.

'We must switch off the shield soon,' warned Osar. 'The energy-drain is too great.'

'What do we do now?' asked Anna.

As usual, everyone looked at Garm, who rubbed an enormous hand across his jaw. 'We could look for an entrance on the far side—but in a building the size of this, we might well lose them completely.' He peered at the jumble of crystal towers and turrets on the screen. 'Somehow we must surprise them . . . Go lower, Tell. I think I see what we need.'

The cruiser swooped down towards the Palace.

Following as they were in Kevin's footsteps, the Kaldor naturally ran into all the same obstacles. They dealt with them with ruthless efficiency.

When they reached the banks of the moat that guarded the Palace, Zargon snapped an order to the ranks of guardsmen. They took components from their battle-packs and rapidly assembled them into a rocket launcher. A series of grapnels carrying fine plastic ropes were fired across the moat and into a wall on the far side where they held fast, gripped by molecular adhesion. In a matter of minutes a simple suspension bridge had been constructed, a rope to walk on, another to hold on to. At a nod from Zargon, one of the guardsmen began edging his way across the bridge. He was just about halfway when a huge fanged head erupted from the water and plucked him from the bridge.

The monster didn't stand a chance. Two heavy laser-cannon were already set up on the bank. There was a crackle of energy and the purple glare of the laser-beams. The lizard-monster gave one shattering roar of rage and pain, then it was blasted into bloody fragments. The surface of the canal boiled and hissed, and a dull red cloud stained the murky waters. There was a brief seething and bubbling, as smaller creatures devoured the shattered remnants of the great beast.

The man in the creature's mouth had died with the monster that attacked him. Kiro and Zargon showed no concern at losing one of their men. After all, thought Jan, they could always go back to the cloning tank and grow another.

Kiro barked an order, and a second guard stepped unhesitatingly onto the bridge. If there were more creatures in the moat they had been frightened off. The second guard reached the other side in safety. Jan, Kiro and Zargon crossed after him and the rest of the guards followed. They marched through the archway and across the courtyard.

The robot trundled out to meet them. 'STOP. YOU ARE NOW ENTERING A HIGH SECURITY ZONE. PLEASE PRODUCE YOUR PASS AND HOLD IT BEFORE MY SCANNER.'

Zargon deactivated the robot with a casual shot from his hand-blaster. The robot staggered back, the purple laser beam playing about its metal body. The shutter in its chest slid back, but a second blast from Zargon exploded its energy-core before it could fire. Smoke pouring from its shattered chest-unit, the robot crashed to the ground like a metal tower.

'YOU ARE INTERFERING WITH MY AUTHORISED FUNCTION,' it protested feebly. 'I SHALL REPORT YOUR ACTION TO CENTRAL CONTROL. YOU ARE LIABLE TO A FINE . . .'

A final shot from Zargon blasted it into silence. 'Primitive technology—but well made to have functioned for so long.' Booted feet ringing on the paving stones, the Kaldor marched into their Palace.

Since Zargon was using an energy sensor as a guide they followed the same route as Kevin once again. The cleaning robot had moved on to another section of corridor by the time they arrived. At a command from Zargon, the guard with the laser-cannon blasted it on sight. The little robot exploded into a shower of metal fragments, its long task ended at last. 'Probably just a low-grade service robot,' said Zargon. 'But it is as well to be sure.'

They went on their way. Eventually they came to the glowing green door, passed through it as Kevin had done and found themselves on the fringes of the indoor jungle.

The guards formed themselves into ranks and stood waiting. During all this time the Kaldor guards had shown no surprise, no fear, no excitement, no interest at all in the many wonders they had encountered.

Perhaps it was because they were clones, thought Jan. But then, Kiro and Zargon reacted, or rather failed to react, in exactly the same way. Maybe all the Kaldor lacked the capacity for surprise, or excitement or wonder. Instead they made do with ruthless efficiency, that and a certain cold pleasure in wanton destruction.

Zargon was studying the energy detector. 'Our way lies straight ahead.

'There is no path,' objected Kiro.

'Then we shall make one.' More snapped orders, and the guards assembled another device, a squat laser gun with a wide bell-like muzzle. They fired and a broad flat beam of light blasted a long smoking path through the jungle. The air was full of smoke and the acrid stink of charred vegetation.

The guards moved the device to the far end of the charred strip and fired again, extending the path.

Leaving their usual trail of destruction, the Kaldor blasted their way through the jungle and Jan, his face cold and expressionless, marched beside them.

By the time his aerial journey ended, Kevin was dizzy and sick. It was like being in a shopping bag that some giant was swinging through the air. At last he was dumped with a thud onto something soft and springy. For a time his surroundings continued to spin around him.

Things steadied at last and he was able to look about him. He was on some kind of wooden platform high in the trees. There was a big hut built on the platform, a kind of tree house, and Kevin in his net had been dumped like a parcel in front of the door. There were more houses, similar but smaller, in the trees nearby.

Grouped around him in a circle were his captors. They were huge grey apes. As his head slowly cleared Kevin was able to get a better look at them. They were quite unlike any ape he had seen on Earth. Their general appearance was like that of a baboon, the size was that of a giant gorilla. They had the brown mournful eyes of chimpanzees, and they chattered gutturally amongst themselves, prodding and poking at Kevin with long, bony fingers.

Something else distinguished them from the apes of Earth. They were carrying weapons. Kevin saw bows, spears, stone-headed clubs, knives made from scraps of jagged metal. One of them even had a blaster though from the lumpy misshapen look of the weapon it had been used as a kind of club.

Kevin wondered what they were planning to do with him. Sacrifice? Or dinner? Weren't the great apes vegetarians? He peered into the gloomy doorway of the hut. It looked rather like Tarzan's tree house in the old Johnny Weismuller movies he'd seen on television. Maybe Tarzan would come out in a loincloth and say 'Me, Tarzan, you Kevin.' Perhaps Jane would appear with a bowl of fruit. They could all go swimming. Kevin decided he must be suffering from delayed shock.

A figure appeared in the doorway. It was an ape like the others, but larger, and its fur was completely white. Its arms and body bore the scars of many battles, and a tattered strip of rainbow-coloured material hung proudly from its shoulders. Something told Kevin he was in the presence of Royalty.

He decided to try and make a good impression.

'Greetings, your majesty. My name is Kevin.'

The ape regarded him unblinkingly. Then to Kevin's astonishment it tapped itself on the chest and said, 'Arko.' It shot out an astonishingly long arm and jabbed Kevin in the chest. 'Why come?'

Using only the simplest words and phrases, talking slowly and emphatically, Kevin told of his capture by the Kaldor and his later escape.

Arko listened impassively. 'Why Kaldor come? What want?'

'Something tremendously important,' said Kevin urgently. 'Some secret that will give them tremendous power. It's hidden on this planet, perhaps even in this jungle. Whatever it is, you mustn't let them have it.'

'Not give?'

'No. The Kaldor are evil ruthless killers. They'll use this thing to seize control over the rest of the Galaxy. They'll plunder your world, and mine and a million others.'

'What Secret? You know?'

Kevin shook his head.

'I know,' grunted Arko. 'Kaldor want Godstone.'

'What will you do?'

'Kill them. All who seek to steal Godstone must die.'

An ape swung onto the platform, fell before Arko and made a long chattering speech. An angry snarling went up from the listening warriors, until Arko stilled them, with a guttural command. A little stiffly, the old ape swung himself upright, using his immensely long arms rather like crutches. He leaped from the platform and stood poised on a nearby branch.

'What's happening?' shouted Kevin. 'Where are you going?'

'Kaldor come with warriors, thunderbolt weapons. We kill them.'

'What about me?'

'Kill you too—sacrifice to Godstone!'

Arko led his warriors off, giving a harsh screaming cry as he swung away.

For a time the trees around were thick with rushing figures as the apes from the tree-village answered the summons of their king. Kevin saw them swinging through the bushes in grey-furred troupes, their weapons clutched incongruously in monkey hands. The noise of movement died away at last and everything was quiet.

Kevin was left on the platform, alone and unguarded. Perhaps the apes thought no one but themselves could travel through the trees. For anyone but a skilled climber, the tree-house was as good as a prison. But Kevin *was* a good climber and he had no intention of waiting here until Arko came to kill him.

The trouble was—he was still trussed up in the net. Kevin tried biting the ropes but they were far too tough for his teeth.

By standing upright he found he could manage a kind of hopping motion inside the net. He made his way inside the hut and looked around. Luckily there was no one else about. Kevin reckoned the place was probably sacred ground, somewhere only the King himself was allowed to enter. The hut was furnished with a few scattered hides, the floor littered with bones and scraps of fruit. A crudely made wooden throne stood in one corner—and across it lay a sword.

Kevin hobbled over. It was less of a sword, he saw, than a giant knife and it was bright and clean, obviously polished with loving care. No doubt it was part of Arko's royal regalia. Maybe he knighted particularly deserving apes with it on state occasions.

Kevin reached out between the meshes, grasped the handle and began slashing at the net. The blade must have been razor-sharp, because the tough ropes fell apart like cobwebs beneath its touch.

Free at last, Kevin kicked aside the net and stood upright. He reached out to lay the sword back on the throne, then hesitated. It was the only weapon he had. On impulse he hunted round behind the throne. Sure enough there was a sheath as well. He slid the blade carefully into the sheath and fixed it to the belt of his Kaldor uniform. Cautiously Kevin crept out of the hut. The nearest tree house was some way away. Through its open windows he could see an ape. There was a baby clutching at its breast. Only women and children left—thought Kevin, the males were all off to the wars. Now was his chance. Clutching at a trailing vine he ran forward and launched himself Tarzan-like off the tree-house platform.

11

Ambush

Anna stopped at the bottom of the ramp and looked around. She was standing on a huge flat stone roof, so high up that the grey clouds looked near enough to touch. Garm and Tell followed her down the ramp. It had been decided that Osar would stay with the ship, standing by, ready for take-off. They'd tried to persuade Anna to stay too, but she wasn't having any.

Anna turned to Garm, who was checking over his equipment. 'Where are we?'

'In a space port of course. Where else would one land a space ship?'

Anna looked surprised, and Tell said, 'We are on the roof of the Palace. This was probably the private landing area for the ruler and his court.'

'And the Kaldor?'

'Somewhere below us. You might say we've managed to get on top of them at last.'

Anna groaned at the terrible joke. Garm gave one of his rare smiles. 'Perhaps we shall be able to surprise them. They won't expect us to arrive from above. With luck we may reach their destination before them.' He studied the energy-detecting device. 'Come, we must find a way into the Palace.'

There were low square buildings at the edge of the landing area. They made their way to the nearest. The door was locked, but Garm wrenched it off its hinges. Inside there was a bare stone room. A flight of steps led downwards. The stairs led to a long, long corridor, which ended in a glowing green door.

On the other side of the door was a long railed gallery that curved away into the distance. There was a blue dome studded with blazing arc-lamps high above their heads, and below them was a waving sea of green.

'It is a jungle,' said Garm delightedly. 'There are jungles like this on the world from which I come.' He plucked at the collar of his space-suit as if he wanted to rip it off and swing unencumbered through the trees.

'But we're indoors,' protested Anna. 'You can't have a jungle inside a building.'

'It is a protected environment, a place where plants and animals can live in warmer conditions than those on the surface. Do you not have such places on Earth?'

'You mean it's a greenhouse?' Anna found it hard to imagine a greenhouse on such an enormous scale.

Garm was checking the energy-detector. 'Whatever it is, it holds the Secret we seek. We must find a way down.'

Thankful he hadn't suggested swinging through the trees after all, Anna followed him along the gallery.

They went on and on, fringing the edge of the jungle high above treetop level. Anna began to fear they would eventually walk round the entire dome and finish up where they'd started. They came to a circular hole in the gallery floor. There was a control panel beside it. Anna peered cautiously over the edge. She was looking into a kind of shaft, a chimney lined with gleaming silvery metal. It stretched down and down, so far you couldn't even see the bottom. 'It's a lift shaft—only someone has taken the lift away!'

'It's an anti-grav chute,' said Tell. 'The question is, is it still operational?' He fiddled with the controls.

Garm fished out a handful of oddly-shaped coins and tossed them over the edge of the shaft. Instead of falling they *floated*, sinking down and down until they were too small to see.

Tell still looked worried. 'It may support a handful of Galactic minims—but is the anti-grav field still strong enough to carry me—or more to the point, my giant friend, will it support you?'

'There is an easy way to find out,' said Garm, and stepped off the edge. To Anna's relief he floated gently downward, just like the coins.

Tell said, 'Well, of course, I knew there was nothing to worry about,' and stepped off after Garm, sinking slowly downwards.

'Hey, wait a minute,' shouted Anna. 'I don't trust that thing. Suppose it stops working halfway down?'

But the other two were already on their way. Unless she wanted to stay up there on her own, she had to join them. Closing her eyes tightly, Anna stepped over the edge . . .

She could see Tell dropping down below her, and Garm below him. They drifted gently downward like leaves from a tree, down and down and down . . . It was a pleasant dream-like sensation, and Anna was almost disappointed when the bottom of the shaft came into sight. She saw Garm land and throw himself to one side. Tell landed next—and made the mistake of standing looking upwards . . .

Anna landed round his neck, and their combined

weights pulled them clear of the anti-grav field. They fell in a tangled heap by the side of the shaft.

Garm lifted them up, one in each hand, and set them gently on their feet. They were in a small bare room with a corridor leading off. They followed it, reached another green, transparent door and emerged into the jungle, this time at ground level.

Anna looked apprehensively at the thick green foliage. 'Do we have to go in there? Suppose it's a zoo, and the animals have run wild?'

Garm showed her the energy-detector. The needle pointed straight into the jungle. 'We must go on. I think we are very close now.'

The going became very hard as they went further into the jungle and soon Garm and Tell produced machete-like knives from their belts and began slashing a way through. Anna had only to follow in the path they had cleared, but even so she soon began to find the journey very tiring. The humid air seemed to sap the strength from her body. Tell saw her stumble, slipped a pill from his belt-pouch and handed it to her. Anna swallowed it down, and soon she felt new strength flooding into her. 'Stim-pill,' said Tell. 'Dangerous to take too many though.'

Strengthened by the pill Anna found she could keep up with the others without difficulty. She hurried after them, and crashed straight into Tell who had come to a sudden halt. He turned and put a finger to his lips. 'Why did you stop?' whispered Anna.

'Because he stopped.' Tell pointed. Garm was standing absolutely still, his great body in a crouch, eyes staring unblinkingly ahead.

She saw him shift his grip on the great knife, so that he was holding it by the blade. It was easy to imagine it whirling through the air, thudding into the body of some enemy. Anna shivered, and Tell put his lips close to her ear. 'Don't worry. He can behead a bug at a hundred metres with that thing!'

Garm's arm drew slowly back. Anna followed the direction of his gaze and saw a flash of black and silver through the trees. 'Kaldor,' she whispered.

Tell nodded. 'Garm will deal with him. We can't let him warn the others . . .'

The figure came into sight, Garm's arm flashed down . . . Anna gave a cry of alarm and rushed forward, hurling herself against him, and bouncing off his enormous bulk.

Perhaps she was in time to deflect his aim, or perhaps her shout made his target jump aside. In any event, the knife flashed by Kevin's head and thudded deep into the bole of one of the giant trees.

Kevin stood quite still, too shocked to move. The next minute Anna was hugging him till his ribs hurt. 'Kev, I can't believe it's you. Are you all right?'

There was a confused period of introductions and explanations with everyone talking at once. Anna introduced Tell and Garm and told Kevin about the League and their attempt to foil the Kaldor. Kevin in turn told them of his adventures with the Kaldor and his escape from the ape-men.

'What about Jan?' asked Anna. 'We *saw* him, Kevin. He seemed to have joined the Kaldor.'

'Yes, I think he has,' said Kevin sadly.

'Perhaps he's just playing a part,' said Anna hopefully. 'Or maybe they've brainwashed him.'

'All I know is he took a shot at me when I escaped—and he wasn't brainwashed then.'

Anna was too shocked to answer. Tell said gently, 'We must be on our way. We know the Kaldor are in the jungle now—we must reach the goal before them.'

Tell gave Kevin one of the stim-pills, and Garm produced a flask of fiery cordial to wash it down. 'I sense that the end is near now,' he said. 'Soon we may have answers to much that puzzles us.' In grim silence, the little party continued their journey.

Anna never knew how long their trek through the indoor jungle lasted. She and Kevin trudged on and on, following the slashing machetes of Garm and Tell. In time even the boost of the stim-pills began to wear off. At last Garm came to a halt, waiting for them to reach him. He pointed silently ahead to a point where the jungle thinned out into a clearing. A white-domed building was gleaming through the trees ahead. It seemed to be made of the finest marble, and the jungle around it had been trimmed into a close green carpet. Great statues flanked the entrance door, and reverent hands had garlanded them with fruit and flowers.

Garm looked at the energy-detector. Its dials were locked at the top of their register. 'Whatever we seek is inside that Temple.'

A mocking voice said, 'Quite so. But we are on the same quest—and as you see, we arrived here before you.'

Their excitement at discovering the Temple had dulled their watchfulness. They were surrounded by a ring of armed Kaldor. Their leader said, 'I am Commander Kiro. Zargon is my First Officer.' He looked at Anna. 'I think you know our Observer friend here.'

A tall figure in black and silver came out of the jungle. 'Jan!' cried Anna. 'Are you all right?'

'Perfectly, thank you, Anna. So, you're here then, Kevin? I didn't think you'd make it this far alone. Unfortunately you both seem to have picked the losing side.'

'Jan, no . . .'

'I'm sorry, Anna. The Kaldor are going to be the greatest power in the Galaxy. I'm going to be one of them. Perhaps they'll make me Emperor of Earth.'

'And perhaps they'll kill you when you're no more use to them,' said Kevin bitterly. 'You don't mean to tell me they still believe that story.'

Jan sprang forward and struck him across the face. 'Silence, traitor!'

Garm said quietly, 'Have the Kaldor been inside the Temple?'

Jan shook his head. 'They guessed you were close behind. They decided to wait here and dispose of you first.'

'Then there is still hope,' said Garm. His calmness seemed to enrage the Kaldor leader. 'None for you, mongrels of the League, or for your human friends. We shall execute you now.'

Furiously Kiro turned to the nearest guard. 'Kill them.'

The guard raised his laser-rifle.

12

Battle in the Jungle

Suddenly Jan stepped in front of the laser-rifle. 'No, Kiro. The humans are traitors to my planet—and I claim the right to execute them myself!'

Kiro hesitated. But the ruthlessness of the sentiment appealed to his Kaldor mind. What better way for Jan to prove his loyalty than by killing his fellows? He nodded, and Jan snatched the laser-rifle from the nearest guard. A flicker of doubt passed through the Kaldor's mind. He decided to ignore it. It would be interesting to see if the Earthman would really kill his companions. And if he did not, what could he do against a squad of armed guards?

Kiro soon learned the answer to that question. Suddenly Jan was behind him, swinging his body round as a shield. The muzzle of the laser-rifle was jammed under Kiro's jaw with painful force. 'Now tell your guards to lay down their blasters. They're not afraid to die, Kiro—but you are.'

Nobody moved. Jan tightened his grip round the Kaldor's throat. 'I mean it. If they fire, I'll blow your head off—and Zargon's next. Now, tell them to drop those blasters.'

The guards stood motionless, their eyes fixed on Kiro. He knew they would shoot or surrender, just as he ordered. The bitterness of defeat rose in his throat like acid. He was about to issue the order for surrender when an arrow took him in the chest and he slumped dead in Jan's arms. More arrows began zipping out of the jungle.

The Kaldor guards might lack individual initiative, but they were trained soldiers for all that, and their response to sudden attack was immediate and unthinking. Ignoring both Jan and their dead leader, they swung round, formed themselves into a defensive semicircle and opened fire on their attackers.

Stepping forward Tell raised his arms and bellowed, 'Stop. Do not attack us. We are your friends. We too are enemies of the Kaldor—' He broke off cursing, as an arrow thudded into his shoulder.

The attackers were clearly not going to distinguish between one alien invader and another. They were intent on killing everyone on sight.

Jan let the dead Kaldor leader slump to the ground. 'Let's get out of here,' he yelled. 'Back into the jungle.'

Garm's commanding voice held him back. 'No! The Temple. *We must reach the Temple.*'

Killer apes began erupting out of the forest. Arko's people were berserk with rage at the attempted profanation of their Godstone. They hurled themselves upon the Kaldor, slashing at them with knives and axes, hammering them with stone clubs, dropping on their shoulders from the trees and throttling them with long, hairy arms.

The guards fought as one man, as in a sense they were, blasting the attacking ape-men with their superior weapons. Ape after ape died in the purple blaze of the laser-beams. But there were always more, and one by one the Kaldor were being chopped down. Zargon rallied the survivors—until a slavering killer-ape clubbed him down.

Jan and the others made their way through the howling chaos of the battle, avoiding the fighting as best they could, striking back only in self-defence. Tell had drawn his blaster and was firing it over his head, shouting and yelling as if to drive his attackers away by sheer volume of noise. Garm relied on his enormous strength, picking up the attacking apes and hurling them back into the jungle.

Jan and Kevin were ranged on each side of Anna, hurrying her along between them. Jan used his laser-rifle with ruthless efficiency, dodging the attacking ape-men whenever he could, shooting them down when he had to. Kevin had drawn the sword he had stolen from Arko and was waving it round his head ferociously, although he too was reluctant to kill unless he must. An ape-man lunged at him with a spear and Kevin parried and thrust automatically, feeling his sword slide into the muscular hairy body. The ape screamed and fell, Kevin wrenched the blade free and pressed determinedly on.

Inch by inch they fought their way to the Temple, climbed a long flight of steps lined with massive statues, and collapsed gasping beneath the shadowed arches of the Temple doorway. Garm's head was bleeding from a jagged cut and the arrow still projected from Tell's arm. Jan, Kevin and Anna were all unhurt. Dazedly, Kevin thought that it was lucky Arko and his warriors had been too busy killing the Kaldor to notice their escape.

Behind them the slaughter was still going on. A

Kaldor dropped, his skull crushed by a stone axe, another fell choking with an arrow in his chest . . . One by one the Kaldor fell and soon the battle was almost over.

Arko surveyed the litter of black-clad bodies. Throwing his head back he gave a screaming cry of triumph. His warriors joined him in the howl of victory, capering and prancing over the dead bodies of their enemies.

'Ready, old friend,' said Garm. Tell nodded.

Garm closed his mighty hand round the arrow and wrenched it out. Tell gave one agonised gasp, then his mouth clamped shut. Garm took a field-dressing from his belt-pouch, clapped it over the wound and pressure-sealed Tell's tunic back in place. 'Can you go on now?'

Tell's face was pale, but he nodded grimly.

Garm led them into the Temple. Inside, it was one enormous dome, the great arched roof soaring cathedral-like above them. Windows that seemed cut from enormous gem-stones turned the light from the jungle outside into a shower of rainbows. There were alcoves set into the walls, and altars with strangely beautiful statues. Weirdly beautiful jungle landscapes flowed over the walls, so brightly painted that their colours seemed to move and glow.

There was strange alien beauty all around them, but one thing dominated the Temple. In its exact centre was a raised stone dais, and on the dais an enormous throne. On it sat a giant figure, robed in gleaming white, surrounded by a fierce golden light. At first Anna thought it was another statue. But as they moved closer she saw that it was alive. Its arms were folded across its chest, and light gleamed from a golden bracelet set with one enormous stone. Only the slightest rise and fall of the huge chest showed that the being still lived. Its face was incredibly long by human standards, with jutting nose, and a high forehead that contrasted with the brutal jaw. The eyes were closed.

Anna felt she had seen this mighty figure before somewhere, and all at once it came to her. The statues of Easter Island, those incredible monuments left by some long-vanished race. The being before her might have been one of those statues brought to life.

Anna looked round and saw the others staring up at the figure in awe. All except Jan. He had a strange rapt look on his face as he stepped up to the dais and raised a hand in salute. 'Greetings, High One. I come from Earth to claim that which was given.'

The sleeping giant awoke.

The great head rose from the chest and turned slowly to and fro. The eyes opened. The long sad face frowned in concentration. 'Is my long vigil ended at last?' The voice was like thunder rumbling through the sky when a storm is near. The giant leaned forward, studying the little group at the foot of the dais. As the dark eyes peered at them, they felt the strength of the mind behind them like a physical force.

'Three of us come from Old Earth,' said Jan, still in that strange, ringing voice. 'Two are of the younger races, the Heirs of Man. We come to claim the Stone of Power, not in our name, but in theirs.'

The giant rose to his full towering height. 'Then take it,' he thundered. 'Take it that I may be free to die at last.'

'Where are your people?' asked Anna. 'What happened to them?'

'They are gone, all gone,' said the deep sad voice. 'Gone to find a new home in another Galaxy. Our sun was dying, and our planet dying with it. We need sun and warmth and light if we are to live. We built great star ships, and set off to find another home.'

'But you stayed behind?'

'The trust was given. It could not be denied. Millions of years ago in the First Age of man, our people visited Earth. Some of us lived there for a time. When the Great Darkness began to fall the Wise Ones of Earth gave us the Stone in trust.'

Kevin asked curiously, 'What is this stone? What does it do?'

'It resonates with the Web,' said the thunderous voice. 'It receives and amplifies the powers which bind together the Cosmos. It gives its wearer great power of mind and body.'

'Why did the men of Old Earth want to get rid of it?'

'Because no one left on Earth was fit to wear it,' said the giant sadly. 'The Stone of Power magnifies flaws as well as virtues. Some died, some went mad, some became totally evil. It was impossible to destroy, yet too dangerous to use. So they sent it clear across the Galaxy—to us. We are not human. We cannot use the Stone, and it cannot harm us. They said that when the Dark Times were over they would come to reclaim it. We waited and waited but no one came.'

'So when your people left, you stayed behind?'

'I was their King—the responsibility was mine. Before the others left they locked me into this stasis-field, immune from the Power of Time. The field could not be broken until one from Old Earth came and said the Words of Release.'

Jan still had that rapt, exalted look on his face. 'The time of waiting is over.'

The alien slipped the jewelled band from off its wrist and held it out. 'Then take the Stone of Power.'

'No!' screamed a frenzied voice. '*I* will take it.' Zargon staggered forwards. His face was a mask of blood, and his uniform was ragged but the laser-rifle in his hands was rock-steady.

Step by staggering step he made his way to the dais, and climbed the steps. No one moved. Even the giant alien was quite still, the jewelled circlet in his hand. The Kaldor snatched it from him, and thrust it on his own head like a crown. The jewel blazed.

For a moment Zargon stood there, glaring down at them, mad eyes glittering with triumph in the white blood-smeared face. Then with a terrible scream he clawed the circlet from his temples and fell dead across the steps. The jewel faded.

'There is danger in the Stone,' said the giant voice. 'There was madness in his mind, and the madness grew until it killed him. Who will take the stone? Quickly, my time is short.'

'I will take it,' said Jan. It was as though someone else was speaking through him. 'I will take it, but I will not wear it. It must go to the Heirs of Man.' He bent down and plucked the circlet from Zargon's dead fingers. As Jan touched the Stone it glowed briefly into life.

'It is finished,' said the giant. 'I may die at last.'

The golden glow around the throne faded as the stasis-field cut out. The effect of the millions of years of waiting swept down at once upon the giant king. His body arched, went rigid, cracked like sun-baked mud, and shattered into dust that was too fine to see. A great wind swept through the Temple, and every trace of him was gone.

'What happened?' whispered Kevin.

'His task was done,' said Garm. 'He was swept away by the Winds of Time. Now our quest is ended. It is time to go.'

They turned away from the empty throne and left the Temple.

When they appeared outside the Temple, Arko and his people were waiting.

The apes ringed the Temple in an enormous circle. Some had bows, at the ready, arrows already fitted and drawn back to fire. Others held knives and spears and axes, still stained with the blood of the Kaldor. A few had blasters, taken from the bodies of their enemies.

Arko stepped forward, and pointed an accusing finger at Jan. 'You come to steal Godstone—like Kaldor. They died. Now you die also. The Godstone is ours.'

'That's not true,' cried Kevin. 'We have a right to the Stone—it was left here for us. What right have you got to keep it?'

'We were slaves to great ones. Servants, pets. They bring us here, keep us in new jungle. They left planet—we stayed. The magic from the Stone entered our minds. We guarded it, worshipped it. Planet ours now, Godstone too. It will make us great—like the Old Ones. You have blasphemed the Godstone. Now you die.'

As he looked round at the apes, Kevin knew they hadn't a chance, in the coming battle. Their enemies were too many, too savage and determined. Blasters wouldn't save Kevin and his friends, any more than they had saved the Kaldor. Most of them would fall at the first volley of arrows, the others would soon be torn to pieces by the maddened apes. Kevin drew his sword.

Suddenly Jan lifted the circlet with the Stone of Power and placed it on his head, just as Zargon had done earlier in the Temple. He went rigid for a moment and his face distorted. The Stone woke to blazing life, pulsing with an eerie red glow. Jan spoke in a strange ringing voice. 'It is time for the Godstone to go now to those who need it. The Stone has given you wisdom. Use it well. Now we shall go.'

Jan walked steadily towards Arko, the Stone pulsing brilliantly on his forehead. Arko gave a moan of fear and threw himself down. The other apes did the same. Striding between their prostrate bodies, Jan led the way into the jungle towards the gravity shaft.

When they reached the bottom of the shaft, Tell operated the controls to reverse the gravity flow. Stepping inside he floated gently upwards. Anna followed, then Kevin. Garm looked worriedly at Jan. The Stone of Power was still blazing on his forehead. 'It is time to go,' said Garm gently. 'Better take off the Stone.'

Jan looked angrily at him, as if about to refuse. Slowly, very slowly he raised his hands. With a sudden convulsive effort he wrenched the circlet from his brow and handed it to Garm. 'Here take it—but don't wear it. Don't let anyone wear it. Find some other way to use its power.'

Garm nodded understandingly. 'Great is he who can wear the Stone of Power—and greater still is he who has the strength to renounce it.'

Jan rubbed a hand across his forehead. 'For a moment there I thought I wouldn't be able to give it up . . .'

'You have not given it up, not altogether, I think. Some part of its strength will be always with you.'

Jan stepped into the grav-shaft and floated gently upwards. The circlet clutched in one enormous hand, Garm followed him.

The others were waiting anxiously at the top of the shaft. As they hurried across the landing pad towards the ship, the ramp slid out to welcome them.

Anna clutched Kevin's arm. 'Just think—we'll soon be on our way home!'

Anna was wrong. The greatest shock of all was still to come.

Epilogue

Exiled to the Stars

The League star-ship sped away from the dying planet. Osar was busy at his controls, preparing to make the Jump to hyperspace, Garm and Tell were in their crew chairs beside him.

Jan, Kevin and Anna sat on couches, eagerly going over their adventures.

Kevin was studying Jan. He seemed to be his easy-going self again, with nothing of the imposing dignity he had worn with the Stone of Power. Kevin wondered what had happened to Jan in the Temple. It was as though some ancient race-memory had spoken through him. 'You took your time letting me know you were really on our side, didn't you,' said Kevin accusingly. 'What's the idea, taking pot-shots at me?'

'Not to mention threatening to execute us all,' said Anna. 'For a moment I really thought you meant it.'

'Just a bit of brilliant acting,' said Jan modestly. 'And as for you, Kev, you may be the great thinker, but the next time you decide on a little action, just be sure to check it out with me first.'

'What do you mean?' said Kevin indignantly. 'Who got the energy-detector away from the Kaldor?'

'Leaving the Kaldor was a good idea,' admitted Jan. 'Grabbing their detector was a good idea too—but not the way you did it. Running away down a nice straight street, with a squad of Kaldor guards right behind you!

The minute Zargon saw you moving you were dead. Where did that leave me? If I ran after you, I was dead. If I stayed where I was, I was dead too—guilty by association. All I could do was grab the laser-rifle and try to convince them I was really on their side. I deliberately shot above your head . . . It worked, too, just about.'

'I suppose threatening to execute us was just another bit of convincing detail.'

'It was the only way to get my hands on a laser-rifle. Everything would have been fine, if your hairy friends hadn't decided to start a war.'

'Shut up you two,' said Anna. 'The main thing is it's over. We're going home!'

Tell swung round in his chair, and something in his face made Anna shiver. 'What is it? You are taking us home, aren't you?'

Garm said slowly, 'We can certainly take you back to Earth, if you wish.'

'Well of course we wish,' said Jan.

Kevin said, 'There's something wrong, isn't there? Something you haven't told us?'

'There are certain problems . . .' Osar punched up a star-map of the Milky Way. 'The temporal-distortion factor. I tried to tell you when we first left Earth. You see, the ratio of temporal instability to spatial flow . . .' His voice tailed off in mumbled technicalities.

Jan looked at Garm. 'You tell us.'

Garm paused, choosing his words carefully. 'You have made an immensely long journey through the time vortex—from one side of the galaxy clear to the other.' He waved at the huge spiral of stars filling the screen. 'Unfortunately, in continuous vortex travel a certain temporal incongruity occurs. The longer the journey, the greater the distortion.'

Anna stared blankly at him. Tell drew a deep breath and said bluntly, 'In the vortex, ship time moves at a different speed from planetary time. Days on the ship may be months or even years on some distant planet . . .'

At last Kevin understood. 'How long have we been away from Earth—in *their* time?'

Garm looked away. 'Something like a hundred of your years—the price of crossing the Galaxy in a single leap . . .'

'A hundred years,' said Anna. 'All our friends will be gone . . . and our parents—' she broke off.

'Suppose you do take us back?' asked Kevin. 'What do we tell the people of that time—about what happened to us?'

'You will be unable to tell them anything,' said Garm. 'We would be forced to erase that part of your memories.' He paused. 'There is an alternative.'

'Well?'

'Return to Galactic Centre with us. We need your help in the struggle against the Kaldor. Now that you know their ways . . .'

'The Kaldor? Didn't we just deal with them?' asked Jan.

'One plot has come to nothing, but there are whole worlds full of Kaldor, all planning future conquest.'

'You would receive a tremendous welcome at Galactic Centre,' Tell said persuasively. 'The leaders of a thousand worlds would come to honour those who came to help the League defeat the Kaldor. No reward will be too great.'

'The only reward I want is to go home again,' said Anna.

Hesitantly Osar said, 'There are many great scientists working at Galactic Centre. Experiments in vortex travel are being conducted all the time. Perhaps someone will know of a way to return you to Earth without the time-lag . . .'

Anna felt a surge of renewed hope. 'So we might be able to get back to Earth in our own time after all?'

'Infinite is the Web,' said Garm softly. 'All things are possible to its Power.' His tone changed. 'If a way exists, we shall find it. We owe you much.'

Tell's face was one broad smile. 'Indeed we do.' He made a gesture of salute. 'Lord Jan, Lord Kevin, the Lady Anna . . . three legendary heroes from Old Earth!'

'That's ridiculous,' said Anna almost angrily. 'You know we're not heroes. We just got mixed up in this by chance.'

'You underestimate yourself, Anna,' said Garm quietly. 'You crossed the Galaxy to help your friends. Kevin tricked the Kaldor, and gave us time to defeat them. Jan spoke the Words of Release, wore the Stone of Power, and then gave it up. Yes, I think you may well be called heroes.'

There was a long silence, as they tried to get used to the thought that the Earth they had known might be lost to them forever.

'Well,' said Jan finally, 'I guess we'll just have to make the best of it. Anyway, I always wanted to be famous.'

Osar was bouncing in his hammock with excitement, and Anna wondered how she could ever have found him frightening. 'So it is agreed? You will come with us to Galactic Centre?'

Kevin answered for all three. 'Yes, we'll come.' He felt a mounting sense of excitement overcoming his sadness. The Galaxy lay before them, unimaginably huge and varied, packed with wonders no one from Earth had seen for millions of years. They had enemies to defeat, good friends to help them in their battles.

Anna was looking sadly at the star map on the vision screen. One little solar system, lost amongst millions of others. One tiny planet, a grain of sand on an infinite beach . . . The picture blurred and vanished, as the starship made the Jump to hyperspace.

They were on their way.